WOK COOKBOOK FOR BEGINNERS

SIMPLE & DELICIOUS RECIPES FOR BEGINNERS TO ENJOY WITH YOUR FAMILY AND FRIENDS | INCLUDING 28-DAYS COMPLETE MEAL PLAN

BY POULA RAY

© Copyright 2022 by Poula Ray - All rights reserved.

This document is geared towards providing exact and reliable information in regards to the topic and issue covered. The publication is sold with the idea that the publisher is not required to render accounting, officially permitted, or otherwise, qualified services. If advice is necessary, legal or professional, a practiced individual in the profession should be ordered.

- From a Declaration of Principles which was accepted and approved equally by a Committee of the American Bar Association and a Committee of Publishers and Associations.

In no way is it legal to reproduce, duplicate, or transmit any part of this document in either electronic means or in printed format. Recording of this publication is strictly prohibited and any storage of this document is not allowed unless with written permission from the publisher. All rights reserved.

The information provided herein is stated to be truthful and consistent, in that any liability, in terms of inattention or otherwise, by any usage or abuse of any policies, processes, or directions contained within is the solitary and utter responsibility of the recipient reader. Under no circumstances will any legal responsibility or blame be held against the publisher for any reparation, damages, or monetary loss due to the information herein, either directly or indirectly.

Respective authors own all copyrights not held by the publisher.

The information herein is offered for informational purposes solely, and is universal as so. The presentation of the information is without contract or any type of guarantee assurance.

The trademarks that are used are without any consent, and the publication of the trademark is without permission or backing by the trademark owner. All trademarks and brands within this book are for clarifying purposes only and are the owned by the owners themselves, not affiliated with this document.

Table of Contents

INTRODUCTION		6
CHAPTER 1:	FUNDAMENTALS OF THE WOK	7
SELECT THE BEST WOK FOR YOU		7
RECOGNIZE THE CORRECT TEMPERATURE		7
SEPARATE THE RECIPES		7
BEFORE YOU START COOKING, CLEAN THE WOK'S SURFACE		7
LOOK, STIR-FRYING ISN'T THE ONLY WAY TO COOK		8
IT'S SIMPLE TO TAKE CARE OF YOUR WORK		8
CHAPTER 2:	WOK DIET	9
A HEALTHIER DIET		9
IMPROVED FOOD TASTE		9
DISPOSAL OF UTENSILS		9
COST-EFFECTIVE		9
EASY COOKING		9
ADDITIONAL FOOD		10
PREPARATIONS ARE SIMPLE		10
KEEP NUTRIENT LOSS TO A MINIMUM		10
CHAPTER 3:	TOOLS NEEDED	11
TONGS OR CHOPSTICKS		11
CLEAVER		11
WIDE SPATULA		11
STEAMERS		11
STRAINER OR SLOTTED SPOON		12
CHOPPING BOARD		12
BAMBOO STEAMER		12
CHAPTER 4:	RECIPES	13
RECIPE 1:	AVOCADO CHICKEN STIR-FRY	13
RECIPE 2:	BOK CHOY STIR-FRY	14
RECIPE 3:	BACON-WRAPPED HOT DOGS	15
RECIPE 4:	BASIL CHICKEN STIR-FRY	16
RECIPE 5:	BEEF AND BROCCOLI	17
RECIPE 6:	BEEF AND LETTUCE CURRY	19
RECIPE 7:	BEEF KALDERETA	20
RECIPE 8:	BEEF LO MEIN	22
RECIPE 9:	BEEF WITH ORANGE PEEL	23
RECIPE 10:	BITTER MELON AND BLACK BEAN SAUCE BEEF	24
RECIPE 11:	BLACK BEAN DRIED TOFU AND GARLIC SCAPES	26
RECIPE 12:	BOK CHOY WITH CRISPY TOFU	27
RECIPE 13:	BONELESS CHICKEN AND TOMATO CURRY	28
RECIPE 14:	BRAISED CHICKEN WINGS	29
RECIPE 15:	BRAISED GREEN BEANS AND POTATOES	31
RECIPE 16:	BRAISED ZUCCHINI	32
RECIPE 17:	BROCCOLI AND BEEF NOODLES	33
RECIPE 18:	CARAMELIZED PORK BELLY	34
RECIPE 19:	CARROT PEAS PAPAYA CURRY	35
RECIPE 20:	CASHEW CHICKEN	36
RECIPE 21:	CASHEW CHICKEN STIR-FRY	37

RECIPE 22:	CAULIFLOWER CURRY	38
RECIPE 23:	CHICKEN AND PRAWN CHOW MEIN	39
RECIPE 24:	CHICKEN HOT POT	41
RECIPE 25:	CHICKEN LETTUCE WRAPS	42
RECIPE 26:	CHICKEN STIR FRY NOODLES	43
RECIPE 27:	CHILI-GARLIC TOFU PUFFS AND MIXED VEGETABLES	44
RECIPE 28:	CITRUS CARP	45
RECIPE 29:	CLASSIC MONGOLIAN BEEF	46
RECIPE 30:	COCONUT CURRY CABBAGE	48
RECIPE 31:	COCONUT CURRY SHRIMP	49
RECIPE 32:	COCONUT SHRIMP	50
RECIPE 33:	CRISPY FRENCH FRIES	51
RECIPE 34:	CRISPY STEAMED DUCK	52
RECIPE 35:	CURRIED CHICKEN WINGS	53
RECIPE 36:	DEEP-FRIED SALMON AND MISO WONTONS	54
RECIPE 37:	DRY-FRIED CAULIFLOWER	55
RECIPE 38:	EGG CURRY IN COCONUT MILK	56
RECIPE 39:	EGG DROP SOUP	58
RECIPE 40:	FIERY PEPPER CHICKEN	59
RECIPE 41:	FRIED BROWN RICE	61
RECIPE 42:	FRIED MUSHROOMS WITH BABY CORN	62
RECIPE 43:	FRIED PORK CHOPS WITH ONION	63
RECIPE 44:	GARLIC CHICKEN	65
RECIPE 45:	GINGER BROCCOLI	66
RECIPE 46:	GINGER GOLDEN CHICKEN CURRY	67
RECIPE 47:	KALE AND BELL PEPPER FRITTATA	68
RECIPE 48:	KUNG PAO CHICKEN	69
RECIPE 49:	KUNG PAO POTATOES	71
RECIPE 50:	LIME FRY	73
RECIPE 51:	LION HEAD MEATBALLS	74
RECIPE 52:	LONG LIFE NOODLES	76
RECIPE 53:	LOTUS LEAF WRAPS	77
RECIPE 54:	MANDARIN PORK STIR-FRY	79
RECIPE 55:	MUSHROOM PEPPER STEAK	80
RECIPE 56:	ORANGE PEEL BEEF	82
RECIPE 57:	OYSTER MUSHROOM	83
RECIPE 58:	PEKING DUCK	84
RECIPE 59:	PORK AND BAMBOO SHOOTS	85
RECIPE 60:	PORK FRIED RICE	86
RECIPE 61:	PORK WITH VEGGIES	87
RECIPE 62:	POTATO CHIPS	88
RECIPE 63:	POTATO CURRY WITH TAMARIND	89
RECIPE 64:	POTATO STIR FRY	91
RECIPE 65:	RED FISH CURRY SOUP	92
RECIPE 66:	SALMON AND NOODLE STIR FRY	93
RECIPE 67:	SATAY VEGGIE NOODLES	94
RECIPE 68:	SAVORY STEAMED EGG CUSTARD	95
RECIPE 69:	SHANGHAI SPRING ROLLS	96
RECIPE 70:	SHIITAKE MUSHROOMS WITH SPRING ONIONS	97
RECIPE 71:	SHRIMP AND CABBAGE STIR-FRY	98
RECIPE 72:	SHRIMP AND SQUID STIR-FRY WITH BOK CHOY	99
RECIPE 73:	SHRIMP LO MEIN WITH BROCCOLI	100
RECIPE 74:	SHRIMP WITH LOBSTER SAUCE	102
RECIPE 75:	SIRLOIN STIR-FRY WITH RAMEN NOODLES	103
RECIPE 76:	SMOKED-TEA TILAPIA	104
RECIPE 77:	SOUP DUMPLINGS	105
RECIPE 78:	SPICY HONEY SESAME CHICKEN AND BROCCOLI STIR-FRY	107

Recipe 79:	Spicy Poached Beef	108
Recipe 80:	Spicy Tempeh Fries	109
Recipe 81:	Spicy Vegetable Lo Mein	110
Recipe 82:	Spinach and Glass Noodle Salad	112
Recipe 83:	Steamed Pork Dumplings	113
Recipe 84:	Steamed Tempeh with Chinese Broccoli in Hoisin Sauce	114
Recipe 85:	Sticky Rice Pork Balls	115
Recipe 86:	Stir-Fried Bok Choy and Mushrooms	116
Recipe 87:	Stir-Fried Pork with Sweet Bean Paste	117
Recipe 88:	Sui Mai Dumplings	118
Recipe 89:	Tea-Smoked Tofu with Sweet Peppers and Red Onions	119
Recipe 90:	Thai Shrimp Stir-Fry	120
Recipe 91:	Tiger Skin Long Hot Peppers	121
Recipe 92:	Tofu and Spicy Tomato Sauce	122
Recipe 93:	Tofu and Veggie Scramble	123
Recipe 94:	Tofu Mapo	124
Recipe 95:	Tofu with Black Bean Sauce	125
Recipe 96:	Twice-Cooked Chile Pork	126
Recipe 97:	Vegetable Fried Rice	127
Recipe 98:	Vegetable Peking Style Dumplings	128
Recipe 99:	Vegetable Pot-Stickers	129
Recipe 100:	Zucchini Frittata	130

Conclusion 131

1. Introduction

When the word WOK cooking is mentioned, most people always visualize a big WOK wielded above an intense flame by a chef. One also envisions Chinese comfort food when the Wok is mentioned, and you don't blame them because the Chinese and the Asians are known for using Wok to prepare healthy meals.

WOK was used in the olden days by our aged parents and if you can recall the taste of the food prepared then and now are very different. When you think about those comfort foods you ate in time past, some images accompany your thoughts, including the picture of you and your family sitting and eating together in the comfort of your home.

While it is true that it is a mystery how the Asian chefs prepare all their ingredients with ease, some of the chefs today don't have the time to craft their meals with Wok meticulously. However, WOK stir-frying happens to be one of the best and easiest ways of preparing your meal, and the best part is, the taste you get from meals prepared with a wok is heavenly. Furthermore, meals prepared using a wok has their Nutritional Information: intact. Maybe that is why our parents lived longer without any complicated health issues.

In recent times, you get to see people suffering from obesity, heart diseases, etc. and when you ask the cause of such illness, what you get most of the time is cholesterol. Most people try to keep fit by skipping meals, which becomes detrimental to their health at the end of the day. However, you can be confident that you will begin to eat healthily and stay healthy with a wok.

If this is actually your first time wanting to use a wok, you can start with the Chinese Wok because it is deep and comes in a bowl-like shape, and it makes sure that your ingredients remain in the middle, which is at the point where the heat is more concentrated.

This WOK cookbook for beginners introduces you to healthy, nutritious, and easy-to-prepare wok recipes, especially if your first time using a WOK.

Chapter 1: Fundamentals of the Wok

• Select the Best Wok For You

Although in a family, a decent wok is vital, it is advisable to choose the appropriate wok based on the kind of stove you own at home. For example, when using an electric burner, the sort of wok to use is different from a gas flame stove. You may also choose them based on the kind of substance they contain. Many people like Chinese carbon steel woks because they heat up and cool down rapidly. Consider the handles, whether you want one long handle or two ear handles, depending on your needs. Fortunately, woks are quite solid and secure, and one with a diameter of at least 12 inches is ideal for use at home.

• Recognize the Correct Temperature

Suppose you need a traditional stir-fry but don't have a wok. It's preferable to do it in a very high heat setting. As a result, based on the dish you're creating, increase the heat to achieve the greatest results. A little smoke or hissing isn't as terrible when you're doing a stir fry. Before adding your spices, make sure your oil isn't too hot. As a result, you'll want to season the wok to prevent the aromatics from clinging to the wok rather than merging with your food. If you like chives, garlic, and other tastes, add the oil following seasoning to extract their flavor without burning after increasing the heat.

• Separate the Recipes

When you have recipes that cook at various speeds, you must prepare them separately. Suppose you have some meat pieces and some crunchy veggies, for example. Instead of cooking them all at once, consider integrating the veggies towards the finish to get the best of both worlds. After that, add the meat and serve, as they've both cooked thoroughly. As a result of the modified time, you won't have a problem with one being overdone and the other being raw. Also, avoid duplicating the recipes if you wish to prepare extra meals. It's better to repeat a process than to stir-fry a large amount of food since not all of it will receive that scorching heat. Optionally, if you're cooking for a large group, don't make it all a stir fry since it's tedious. Make a stew, divide the rice, and prepare some cold foods.

• Before You Start Cooking, Clean the Wok's Surface

When cooking in a wok, it's usually a good idea to season your surface beforehand. Your food will not cling to the surface as a result of this. For example, if you're preparing chicken and it adheres to the pan, it'll burn before the entire thing is done. As a result, not only will the taste of the meal alter, but it will also be difficult to move the remainder of the dish around the wok. As a result, make your wok nonstick by pouring oil into the wok before cooking and emptying it into a heat-proof container as soon as it reaches smoking temperatures. Following that, add some new cooking oil, which will make it easier for you to flip and toss the meal around.

- **Look, Stir-Frying Isn't the Only Way to Cook**

The wok is highly cost-effective since it can be used more than just stir-frying. It's ideal for deep frying since it uses far less oil than a frying pan. You may also use it to create stews, boil water, and smoke food. Others use it to steam food, for example, by placing a bamboo steamer inside the wok. You may also steam by placing metal trivets in the bottom of a wok, placing a dish on top of the trivet, and covering it. All of this is feasible with a wok, and you may enjoy a variety of delectable foods as soon as you understand how to prepare them.

- **It's Simple to Take Care of Your Work**

The wok is a ubiquitous piece of cookware in Chinese households. As a result, they understand how to properly care for it. Suppose you're using it for the first time. To begin with, they are unbreakable, so you can give them a thorough cleaning if they need it. However, after it's clean, don't forget to season it. You'll need a scoop for removing the stock water and oil as part of wok maintenance since it's better than most tools that may chip the wok's surface. The bamboo brush is also useful for cleaning plates while the food is still hot. Make sure all bristles are of good quality and won't melt. The slotted spoon or ladles are also useful items when using a wok.

Chapter 2: Wok diet

The most typical application for a wok is stir fry. However, its one-of-a-kind design allows for a wide range of uses. Because it is so deep, it may be filled with water to cook meals and oil for deep-frying. A wok may be used to smoke meats and cheeses when paired with a rack or wood chips. A cover may be added to the wok to steam vegetables and seafood.

Below are the benefits of a wok. Various frying pans are used for steaming, boiling, stir-frying, braising, and cooking soup in Chinese cuisine. It differs from conventional pans because it is curved, altering the cooking process.

- ## A Healthier Diet

A balanced diet and also the healthy eating habits are vital for everyone. Woks benefit from cooking with less oil, making them healthier and easier to digest. Dishes may be made more quickly while retaining the firm texture of meats and veggies.

- ## Improved Food Taste

You may have heard that woks may improve the flavor of your food. You can blend tastes and include additional ingredients without changing the original. On the other hand, overcooking may lead food to lose its taste and even cause it to be ruined; a frying pan reduces this risk by making meal preparation quick.

- ## Disposal of Utensils

A wok is multipurpose cooking equipment that may be used for deep-frying, sautéing, steaming, and deep-frying, among other things. It makes cleaning up your kitchen a lot simpler.

- ## Cost-Effective

To acquire frying pans, you'd think you'd need a lot of loans; however, the pricing of woks on the internet will astound you. To get better outcomes, you should use high-quality woks. Take into consideration that several excellent high-quality woks are reasonably priced. There is a wide range of first-rate models available to suit any budget. The cost of an electric one is higher. They're also far more expensive than standard frying pans.

- ## Easy Cooking

The meats or vegetables that have taken the longest to cook are fried inside the hot oil at the bottom of the wok. Blend in the fricasseed when it's nearly done. Other ingredients like fish and vegetables are introduced after the meat or veggies have been forced up to the edges of the pan. While the delicate food cooks, the hard food cooks. However, they do cook once at a slower rate to prevent overcooking. The wok's unusual structure allows you to cook meat and veggies more evenly.

- ### **Additional Food**

Woks are fantastic for foodies. Because of their high edges, woks enable cooking to be more accessible. It allows you to cook more food. You can prepare more of your favorite dishes while still having leftovers for the following day. Food is much less likely to fall onto the burner, making it simpler to clean the kitchen.

- ### **Preparations are Simple**

You'll notice that the cooking will be considerably more efficient than before. You cook quicker because of two things. Mixed-fried food is often easy to make. The dish is swiftly cooked in little quantities of oil and sauces before being served. The design of the wok is the second factor; it ensures that heat is spread more effectively through the base of a frying pan, resulting in faster cooking times.

- ### **Keep Nutrient Loss to a Minimum**

Cooking food for a prolonged time might eliminate nutrients such as vitamin C and B. In a modest quantity of oil, stir-frying veggies quickly may reduce these losses. Some nutrients will be lost due to the high heat, but not baking, cooking, or roasting vegetables.

Chapter 3: Tools Needed

Besides the fact that you need a WOK, there are other cooking tools that you also need to make your daily Chinese cooking easier than you envisioned. Of course, if you are an expert in cooking already, you might already have these tools, but for beginners' sake, below is a list of the essential tools you will actually need to prepare a fantastic Chinese recipe using your WOK.

Let us start with the rice cooker: a rice cooker is necessary, especially if you want to cook any grain or Chinese food. A rice cooker makes your cooking faster and easier, and it also ensures your food stays warm for a more extended period. A combination of a wok and a rice cooker will make a sumptuous meal within a few minutes.

- **Tongs or Chopsticks**

Cooking a Chinese meal cannot be complete without tongs or chopsticks. Chopsticks or tongs ensure you can move things around with ease. In addition, these cooking chopsticks are long and resistant to heat. However, you can only use chopsticks if you are used to it, but if not, you can decide to use tongs. The basic truth is that employing any of these items will make your cooking procedure easier.

- **Cleaver**

Your Chinese cooking tool cannot be complete without a cleaver. It could be small or big, and it could also be heavy or light with either a carbon-steel blade or a stainless-steel blade and a wooden or metal handle.

Most chefs will always recommend the cleaver with a wooden handle and a stainless-steel blade that is balanced because it can be used for chopping, cutting, mincing, and slicing. The cleaver is a professional knife perfect for almost everything cutting and chopping, thereby making your cutting task more uncomplicated than you think.

- **Wide Spatula**

A spatula is being used all the time, but your wide metal spatula is the best with a wok, mainly when used for fried rice. With the metal spatula, you can easily scrape anything that becomes stuck in your WOK during cooking. However, you can also use the regular spatula for any other meal that doesn't need too much scraping.

- **Steamers**

There are a lot of steamers in the market, but if you can get bamboo steamers, you are good to go. The bamboo steamers are traditional, and they consist of a woven bamboo mesh base, a circular frame, and a shallow bamboo cover. The bamboo steamers also come in various sizes, and you could choose the size that is perfect for you and can comfortably fit into your standard Wok. Do you know you could also stack about 2 or 3 steamers simultaneously? Yes, it makes your cooking easier and faster. Furthermore, if you don't want to get a bamboo steamer, you can choose a stainless-steel steamer that will fit perfectly into your work. However, some stainless-steel steamers also come with a bamboo mesh.

- **Strainer or Slotted Spoon**

Two types of filters are handy for Chinese cooking. One is the steel mesh strainer which comes with a long split bamboo handle, and it ranges from about 4 inches to 14 inches to get the perfect size for you. Then the second type of strainer is a combination of a long metal and hollow handle with a large shallow, sturdy stainless-steel bowl. It also comes with perforated holes and in different sizes as well. With these strainers in your kitchen, cooking will be easier because you can drain quickly and confidently.

- **Chopping Board**

Your kitchen is incomplete without a chopping board. There are a lot of chopping boards in the market that sometimes, one gets confused about the perfect fit for their kitchen.

But among various Chinese cooks, the rubber-like chopping board is ideal for them, and it comes in different sizes and shapes, so you will undoubtedly see the right size for your kitchen and needs. It is more important than making your knife dull, unlike the white plastic chopping board. Of course, you can also go for the wooden cutting board or the laminated bamboo chopping boards; they are also perfect.

- **Bamboo Steamer**

Do you wish to make some lovely dumpling recipes, steamed fish, or any other fantastic dish with your WOK? If so, it would be best if you got a bamboo steamer. The bamboo steamer will enable you to steam your foods according to the amount of time it needs to be steamed and if possible, get a multilayered steamer to steam whatever you want to steam in layers. Bamboo steamers come in different sizes, so you should consider your needs before getting one.

Chapter 4: Recipes

Recipe 1: Avocado Chicken Stir-Fry

Serving Size: 4

Preparation Time: 10 minutes

Cooking Time: 15 minutes

Ingredients:

- 1/2 cups of chicken broth
- 2 cups of snow peas
- 1/4 cup of soy sauce
- 1 tablespoon of cornstarch
- 4 bunches of green onions, cut into 1-inch pieces
- 1 clove of garlic, minced
- 1 tablespoon of vegetable oil
- 2 cups of cremini mushrooms, stems discarded, caps thinly sliced
- 4 skinless, boneless chicken breast halves, bite size pieces
- 2 large ripe but firm avocados - peeled, pitted, and cut into large chunks

Directions:

1. Mix garlic, cornstarch, soy sauce, and chicken broth in a bowl until cornstarch turns smooth, set aside.
2. Place a large-sized skillet or wok on the stove and turn on to medium-high heat. Put oil until sparkling. Stir and cook the chicken for approximately about 5 minutes until meat is no longer pink in the middle and is cooked through. Remove from skillet or wok and set aside. Put snow peas into hot wok or skillet. Stir and cook for approximately about 3 minutes until bright green in color yet still crisp. Mix in the green onions and mushrooms, and cook for approximately about 5 minutes until mushrooms are softened and have given up their juice. Get rid of extra juices, if there is.
3. Put the chicken back to wok. Mix briefly over medium heat to combine with the cooked vegetables. Pour the reserved sauce ingredients to remix, if necessary, and place to the wok. Slowly mix in the avocado, and allow the mixture to bubble for approximately about 3 minutes until the sauce turns thick. Mix slowly to cover everything in sauce, then serve.

Recipe 2: Bok Choy Stir-Fry

Serving Size: 4

Preparation Time: 15 minutes

Cooking Time: 15 minutes

Ingredients:

- 1 teaspoon of sugar
- 4 garlic cloves, thinly sliced
- 600 grams of baby bok choy
- 2 tablespoons of peanut oil
- 2 spring onions, thinly sliced
- 1 piece of fresh ginger, chopped (just about 1 teaspoon)
- 1 teaspoon of coarse sea or kosher salt
- 1/8 teaspoon of ground white pepper

Directions:

1. Cut off a piece from the end of each bok choy head. Slice the bok choy crosswise. Wash the bok choy in cold water in several passes and dry in a colander or salad spinner until dry to the touch.
2. Heat the prepared oil in a wok or large skillet over medium-high heat until hot but not smoking. Add ginger, scallions, and garlic and stir-fry, approximately about 15 seconds.
3. Add the bok choy, salt, sugar and pepper and stir-fry for approximately about 1 minute. Add 1 tablespoon of water and cook, covered, until wilted, approximately about 30 seconds.
1. Remove lid, stir-fry for approximately about 5 seconds and serve.

Recipe 3: Bacon-Wrapped Hot Dogs

Serving Size: 8

Prearation Time: 10 minutes

Cooking Time: 30 minutes

Ingredients:

- 8 hot dogs, preferably natural casing
- 1 white onion, small-sized, diced
- 8 bacon strips, thick-cut
- 1 avocado, ripe, diced
- 8 hot dog buns, steamed or toasted
- 1 small bag of crushed potato chips
- 3 to 4 pickled jalapeño peppers, diced
- Juice of 1 lime, fresh
- 1 tomato, large-sized, diced
- 2 quarts of peanut oil
- 1 cup of mayonnaise
- Kosher salt

Directions:

2. Wrap each hot dog with a bacon strip, preferably in a spiral pattern. Once done, using toothpicks, secure the ends of bacon.
3. Oil and heat the air fryer with peanut oil. Add and cook the hot dogs until the bacon turns crispy. Transfer to a paper towel-lined plate.
4. Combine the avocado with jalapeño, tomato, lime juice & onion in a medium-sized mixing bowl then, season with salt to taste, gently toss the ingredients to combine.
5. Top the hot dogs first with mayonnaise and then, with the avocado mix, followed by crushed chips. Serve immediately and enjoy.

Recipe 4: Basil Chicken Stir-Fry

Serving Size: 6

Preparation Time: 10 minutes

Cooking Time: 15 minutes

Ingredients:

- 5 green onions, sliced
- 2 tablespoons of water
- 1 tablespoon of soy sauce
- 3 cloves of garlic, chopped
- 1 tablespoon of white sugar
- 2 (6-ounce) bags fresh baby spinach leafs
- 4 tablespoons of vegetable oil
- 1 cup of fresh basil, thinly sliced
- 2 pounds of Skinless & boneless chicken breast halves, sliced into small pieces

Directions:

1. Combine sugar, water and soy sauce in a bowl.
2. In the soy sauce mixture, marinate your chicken for approximately about 30 minutes.
3. In a prepared large wok, heat 1 tablespoon of oil over medium heat.
4. Stir in your green onions into oil and cook for approximately about 1 minute. Transfer cooked green onion to a small bowl.
5. Add the 3 remaining tablespoons of oil to wok. Add in your chicken and marinade and cook for approximately about 5-minutes or until chicken is no longer pink in middle.
6. Add your spinach leafs to your chicken and continue to cook for approximately about another 4 minutes while stirring occasionally.
7. Stir in your green onion mixture to chicken and spinach mixture. Continue to cook for approximately about 2 minutes, then add in basil and cook for approximately about another 3 minutes. Serve and enjoy!

Recipe 5: Beef and Broccoli

Serving Size: 4

Preparation Time: 15 minutes

Cooking Time: 20 minutes

Ingredients:

- 1 tablespoon of baking soda
- 1 tablespoon of cornstarch
- Kosher salt
- 4 tablespoons of water, divided
- 2 tablespoons of oyster sauce
- 1 tablespoon of hoisin sauce
- 2 tablespoons of Shaoxing cooking wine
- 2 teaspoons of light brown sugar
- 2 tablespoons of cooking oil
- 4 fresh ginger slices, about the size of a quarter
- 12 ounces of skirt steak, cut across the grain into ¼-inch-thick slices
- 1 pound of broccoli, cut into bite-size florets
- 2 garlic cloves, finely minced

Directions:

1. In a small bowl, mix the beef and baking soda to coat. Set aside for approximately about 10 minutes. Rinse the beef extremely well and then pat it dry with paper towels.
2. In another small bowl, stir the cornstarch with 2 tablespoons of water and mix in the oyster sauce, wine, brown sugar, and hoisin sauce. Set aside.
3. In the wok, heat the oil over medium-high heat until it shimmers. Season the oil by adding the ginger and a pinch of salt. Allow the ginger to sizzle in the oil for approximately about 30 seconds, swirling gently. Add the beef and stir-fry until no longer pink. Transfer the beef to a bowl and set aside.
4. Add the broccoli and garlic and stir-fry for approximately about 1 minute, then add the remaining 2 tablespoons of water.
5. Return the beef to the wok and stir in the sauce for approximately about 2 or 3 minutes, until fully coated and the sauce has thickened slightly. Discard the ginger, transfer to a platter, and serve hot.

Recipe 6: Beef and Lettuce Curry

Serving Size: 4

Preparation Time: 10 minutes

Cooking Time: 22 minutes

Ingredients:

- 3 garlic cloves, minced
- 3 tablespoons of fish sauce
- 3 cups of torn lettuce
- 2 tablespoons of lemon juice
- 2 tablespoons of sesame oil
- 2 cups of canned tomatoes, diced
- 1 cup of uncooked white rice
- 1 tablespoon of chili sauce
- 1 tablespoon of Sriracha sauce

- 1 tablespoon of soy sauce
- 1 pound of ground beef
- 1 cup of Rotel tomatoes
- 1 tablespoon of curry powder
- ¼ cup of white sugar

Directions:

1. In a saucepan of salted water, cook your rice according to the package directions. Drain.
2. Combine the sugar, garlic, fish sauce, chili sauce, Sriracha sauce, and lemon juice with ¼ cup of water.
3. In a pan, heat the sesame oil and cook the garlic cloves for approximately about 2 minutes. Mix in the ground beef and curry powder and stir.
4. Stir in the diced tomatoes and Rotel tomatoes, and ½ the sauce mix.
5. Simmer for approximately about 20 minutes. Stir the torn lettuce into the wok.
6. Serve over the rice and drizzle with the remaining sauce mixture.

Recipe 7: Beef Kaldereta

Serving Size: 4

Preparation Time: 20 minutes

Cooking Time: 1 hour 30 minutes

Ingredients:

- 3 cloves of garlic, crushed
- 2 carrots, thinly sliced
- 1 potato, sliced into small cubes
- 1 green bell pepper, thinly sliced
- 1 yellow onion, chopped
- 1 red bell pepper, thinly sliced
- 1 beef cube, bouillon
- 1, 8 ounce can of tomato sauce
- 5 tablespoon of liver spread
- ¼ teaspoon of red pepper flakes, crushed
- 2 pounds of beef chuck, sliced into small cubes
- Dash of salt and black pepper
- 1 ½ cups of water
- 6 tablespoon of vegetable oil

Directions:

1. Oil and heat the pan, add in the red and green bell peppers. cook for approximately about 3 minutes. Remove and transfer to a plate. Set aside.
2. Add the carrots and potatoes into the wok with the oil. cook for approximately about further 3 to 5 minutes. Transfer to a plate and set aside for now.
3. Add in three spoonfuls of oil. Once the oil is actually hot, add in the crushed garlic and chopped onion. Stir well to mix and cook for approximately about 5 minutes or until golden brown.
4. Add in the beef cubes. cook for approximately about 8 to 10 minutes or until browned.
5. Pour in the water and tomato sauce. Stir to mix and bring this mixture to a boil. Once boiling add in the beef bouillon cube and cover. Reduce the heat to a heat of low and cook for approximately about 1 hour or until the beef is tender.
6. After this time add in the liver spread and season with a dash of salt and black pepper. Add in the cooked potatoes, carrots and bell peppers. Stir well to mix. Cover and continue to cook for approximately about 5 minutes.
7. Add in the crushed red pepper flakes and stir to incorporate. Continue to cook for approximately about 3 minutes.
8. Remove from heat and serve with rice.

Recipe 8: Beef Lo Mein

Serving Size: 4

Preparation Time: 15 minutes

Cooking Time: 25 minutes

Ingredients:

- 1 tablespoon of peanut oil
- 1 teaspoon of dark sesame oil
- 1 (8-ounce) package spaghetti
- 4 cloves garlic, minced
- 1 pound of Flank steak, thinly sliced
- 4 cups of mixed veggies (whatever you like)
- 3 tablespoons of low-sodium soy sauce
- 2 tablespoons of brown sugar
- 1 tablespoon of fresh ginger root, minced
- 1 tablespoon of Asian chile paste with garlic
- 1 tablespoon of oyster sauce

Directions:

1. Boil a prepared large pot of lightly salted water. Cook your spaghetti in the water according to package directions. Once cooked drain noodles and transfer to a large bowl. Drizzle your sesame oil over spaghetti then toss to coat. Put a plate over noodles to keep them warm.
2. In your wok, heat the peanut oil over medium-high heat. Cook and stir prepared garlic and ginger in hot oil until fragrant, approximately about 30 seconds. Add in your mixed veggies, then stir to combine and cook for approximately about 3 minutes or until veggies are slightly tender.
3. Stir in your flank steak to wok and cook for approximately about 5 minutes or until beef is cooked through.
4. Mix brown sugar, soy sauce, chile paste and oyster sauce in a bowl, then pour mixture over spaghetti. Dump spaghetti mixture into wok along with veggies and steak and cook for approximately about 3-minutes or until hot. Serve and enjoy!

Recipe 9: Beef with Orange Peel

Serving Size: 6

Preparation Time: 25 minutes

Cooking Time: 6 hours

Ingredients:

- 1 tablespoon of low-sodium soy sauce
- 1 tablespoon of cornstarch
- 1 tablespoon of peanut oil
- 3 garlic cloves (chopped)
- 1 teaspoon of dark sesame oil
- 1/2 teaspoon of baking powder
- 1 tablespoon of low-sodium soy sauce
- 2 tablespoons of frozen orange juice concentrate, (thawed)
- 1 tablespoon of rice vinegar
- 1 teaspoon of dark sesame oil
- 1 tablespoon of brown sugar
- 600 grams of Beef tenderloin, cut into thin slices
- 1 teaspoon of cornstarch
- 1 tablespoon of chopped fresh ginger root
- 1 tablespoon of finely grated orange zest
- 1/4 teaspoon of red pepper flakes

Directions:

1. Combine the beef, 1 tablespoon of soy sauce, 1 tablespoon of cornstarch, 1 teaspoon of sesame oil, and baking soda in a bowl and mix well. Heat the prepared peanut oil in a wok or large non-stick skillet over high heat and refrigerate for 1 to 3 hours.
2. Stir in the garlic, ginger, orange zest and red pepper flakes and cook it about until the garlic starts to brown, approximately about 20 to 30 seconds.
3. Add the beef; cook and stir until beef is brown and crispy, approximately about 5 minutes.
4. Whisk together 1 tablespoon of soy sauce, concentrated orange juice, rice vinegar, 1 teaspoon of sesame oil, brown sugar, and 1 teaspoon of cornstarch in a small bowl.
5. Stir into the beef and cook until the sauce has thickened and run clear, approximately about 30 seconds.

Recipe 10: Bitter Melon and Black Bean Sauce Beef

Serving Size: 4

Preparation Time: 25 minutes

Cooking Time: 1 hour and 35 minutes

Ingredients:

- 1 bitter melon, seeded and sliced
- 3/4 cup of water
- salt to taste
- 1 tablespoon of oil
- ice cubes
- 1/2 onion, sliced
- 1 tablespoon of chopped fresh ginger
- 1 tablespoon of oyster sauce
- 2 teaspoons of cornstarch, divided
- 6 ounces of beef, sliced
- 1 tablespoon of black bean sauce
- 2 cloves of garlic
- 1/4 teaspoon of baking soda
- 2 teaspoons of soy sauce, divided
- 1 pinch of white sugar, or to taste

Directions:

1. Make an ice bath in a bowl filled with ice and salted water. Meanwhile, fill a large pot with lightly salted water; leave to boil. Place the bitter melon in the boiling water for approximately about 2 minutes or until it turns firm but tender. Strain the bitter melon then transfer to the ice bath for approximately about an hour until the bitterness is extracted. Drain the bitter melon.
2. In a bowl, combine baking soda, a teaspoon of soy sauce, and a teaspoon of cornstarch. Coat the beef with the marinade; leave in the refrigerator for an hour.
3. Set a large saucepan or wok over high heat until smoking. Add in a tablespoon of oil. Cook the marinated beef, approximately about 2 minutes per side or until the slices are browned. Remove the beef then add a teaspoon of oil. When the oil heats up, stir in the ginger, onion, and garlic for approximately about 30 seconds or until fragrant. Add in the bitter melon and stir for approximately about 1 minute.
4. Pour the black bean sauce into the bitter melon mixture. Add in sugar, remaining soy sauce, and oyster sauce and stir. Mix in 3/4 cup of water. Put the lid on the pot; allow to simmer for approximately about 2 to 3 minutes until the flavors are combined. Uncover the pot. Make a slurry with a teaspoon of water and the remaining cornstarch and add the mixture into the pot. Stir until the mixture thickens.

Recipe 11: Black Bean Dried Tofu and Garlic Scapes

Serving Size: 3

Preparation Time: 10 minutes

Cooking Time: 20 minutes

Ingredients:

- 3 tablespoons of canola oil
- 3 tablespoons of water
- ½ teaspoon of sea salt
- 1 teaspoon of minced fresh ginger
- 4 fresh bird's eye chilies, cut into thin rings
- ¼ cup of fermented black beans
- 2 tablespoons of Shaoxing wine
- 2 ½ cups of ¼-inch segments garlic scapes
- 2 tablespoons of Chinese light soy sauce
- 2 teaspoons of granulated sugar
- 1 package of five-spiced dried (pressed) tofu
- ½ teaspoon of ground white pepper

Directions:

1. Cut the dried tofu into ¼-inch cubes.
2. In a wok or large-sized skillet, heat the oil over medium heat. Add the ginger and chili and stir until fragrant.
3. Add the dried tofu, garlic scapes, and fermented black beans. Raise the temperature to high and stir for approximately about 1 minute.
4. Add the wine, soy sauce, sugar, water, salt, and white pepper and cook, stirring constantly, for approximately about another 3 minutes. Remove from the heat and serve hot.

Recipe 12: Bok Choy with Crispy Tofu

Serving Size: 4

Preparation Time: 10 minutes

Cooking Time: 20 minutes

Ingredients:

- 2 tablespoons of chopped, fresh ginger
- 3 tablespoons of cornstarch
- 1 teaspoon of kosher salt
- 2 tablespoons of light soy sauce
- 2 tablespoons of cooking oil
- 3 garlic cloves, crushed and chopped
- 2 cups of sliced bok choy (about 1-inch strips)
- 1 bunch of scallions, both white and green parts, cut into ½-pieces
- 1 pound of extra-firm tofu, drained and cut into ½-inch cubes
- 2 tablespoons of ketchup
- Steamed rice, for serving

Directions:

1. In a large zip-top bag, combine the tofu, cornstarch, and salt. Shake to coat evenly.
2. In the wok, heat the oil over high heat until it shimmers.
3. Add the coated tofu, ginger, and garlic and stir-fry for approximately about 5 minutes, or until the tofu is golden brown.
4. Add the prepared bok choy and stir-fry for approximately about 1 minute, until bright green. Add the scallions and stir-fry for approximately about 30 seconds.
5. In a prepared small bowl, whisk together the soy sauce and ketchup. Add the sauce to the wok and cook, stirring, for approximately about 1 minute, until the tofu and bok choy are evenly coated.
6. Serve over steamed rice.

Recipe 13: Boneless Chicken and Tomato Curry

Serving Size: 4

Preparation Time: 20 minutes

Cooking Time: 35 minutes

Ingredients:

- 1 teaspoon of ginger paste
- 1 teaspoon of cinnamon powder
- 1 teaspoon of paprika
- ¼ teaspoon of turmeric powder
- 1 teaspoon of garlic paste
- ½ teaspoon of salt
- 1 teaspoon of dry coriander powder
- 16 ounces chicken, pieces, boneless
- 4 ripe tomatoes, sliced
- 1 teaspoon of cumin powder
- 2 tablespoons of butter
- 2-3 green chilies

Directions:

1. Melt butter in wok and fry chicken until lightly golden or till no longer pink.
2. Add in ginger garlic paste and stir fry for approximately about 1-2 minutes.
3. Season with salt, paprika, turmeric powder, cinnamon powder, and coriander powder. Mix thoroughly.
4. Transfer tomatoes and green chilies, stir well.
5. Cover with lid and let it cook on medium fame for approximately about 8-10 minutes.
6. Make sure chicken is softened well.
7. Serve and enjoy.

Recipe 14: Braised Chicken Wings

Serving Size: 8

Preparation Time: 20 minutes

Cooking Time: 40 minutes

Ingredients:

- 24 pieces of chicken wings, split
- ½ cup of dark soy sauce, divided
- 3 tablespoon of vegetable oil
- 1 cup of water
- 1 piece of shallot, thinly sliced
- 5 cloves of garlic, smashed
- 3 pieces of whole star anise
- 1 piece of cinnamon stick
- 1 piece of Fresno chili, halved lengthwise
- 2 teaspoons of five spice powder, divided
- cup of unseasoned rice wine
- ½ cup of low-sodium soy sauce
- ¼ teaspoon of Sichuan peppercorns
- 3 tablespoons of ginger, thinly sliced and divided
- 3 pieces of scallions, trimmed and halved crosswise
- ¼ cup of sugar
- ¼ teaspoon of freshly ground white pepper

Directions:

1. Toss chicken together with dark soy sauce, plus half of ginger and five spice powder. Set aside to marinade in the fridge for approximately about an hour.
2. Heat oil in a wok on medium high when the chicken wings are ready and stir fry scallions, shallots, garlic, and remaining ginger. stir for approximately about 2 minutes, then, sprinkle sugar, star anise, cinnamon stick, peppercorns, and white pepper.
3. Pour in the remaining dark soy sauce, plus low-sodium soy sauce, plus water, and let it boil on high.
4. Add chicken wings, discarding marinade, and pour vinegar.
5. Remove wings to a plate with a slotted spoon and pour the liquid through a fine sieve, discarding solids.
6. Return the liquid to a saucepan and simmer on high until thickened and reduced.
7. Put back the chicken wings into the sauce, toss gently, and transfer to a serving platter.
8. Serve and enjoy.

Recipe 15: Braised Green Beans and Potatoes

Serving Size: 5

Preparation Time: 15 minutes

Cooking Time: 20 minutes

Ingredients:

- ¾ cup of water
- ½ teaspoon of sea salt
- 2 medium yellow potatoes
- 3 tablespoons of canola oil
- 4 garlic cloves, minced
- 1 tablespoon of Chinese light soy sauce
- 1 tablespoon of vegetarian oyster sauce
- 2 cups of halved and trimmed green beans
- ½ teaspoon of granulated sugar

Directions:

1. Peel the potatoes and quarter them lengthwise. Roll-cut them into small, bite-size pieces no thicker than ½ inch and 1½ inches long.
2. In a wok or a large skillet, heat the oil over medium-high heat until it just begins to smoke. Add the green beans and stir for approximately about 1 minute. Add the potato and stir for approximately about 2 minutes. Add the garlic and stir for approximately about 1 minute.
3. Add the soy sauce, oyster sauce, salt, sugar, and water. Simmer the potato and green beans uncovered, stirring constantly to make sure all the pieces cook evenly, for approximately about 8 minutes, or until the liquid is reduced and just coating the vegetables.
4. Serve hot.

Recipe 16: Braised Zucchini

Serving Size: 4

Preparation Time: 30 minutes

Cooking Time: 20 minutes

Ingredients:

- 2 tablespoons of sesame oil
- 1/4 cup of water
- 1 small diced yellow onion
- 3 cloves of garlic, chopped
- 4 zucchinis (sliced)
- 1 tablespoon of chopped fresh ginger root
- 1 tablespoon of soy sauce
- 1 tablespoon of Chinese black bean sauce
- 2 Thai chili peppers (seeded and chopped)

Directions:

1. Heat the prepared sesame oil in a wok or large skillet over medium-high heat. Stir the onion and garlic in the hot oil until the prepared onion begins to soften, approximately about 2 minutes.
2. Stir in the black bean sauce and chilies and stir-fry the onions until the onions are coated in the black bean sauce, approximately about 30 seconds.
3. Stir in the zucchini, ginger, soy sauce, and water. Cover and cook the zucchini, ginger, soy sauce and water on medium-low for approximately about 15 minutes, stirring occasionally, until the zucchini is tender.

Recipe 17: Broccoli and Beef Noodles

Serving Size: 4

Preparation Time: 20 minutes

Cooking Time: 50 minutes

Ingredients:

- 1 tablespoon of Sriracha
- 3 minced garlic cloves
- 2 fresh limes, juice & wedge-cut
- 1 floret-cut large broccoli head
- 1 teaspoon of honey, pure
- 12 ounces of noodles, udon or rice, wide
- 1/3 cup of soy sauce, reduced sodium
- 3 tablespoon of oil, toasted sesame
- 1 tablespoon of corn starch
- 3/4 pound of thinly sliced flank steak
- 8 ounces of sliced mushrooms, baby Bella

Directions:

1. Bring a large-sized pot of lightly salted, filtered water to boil. Add noodles and cook using instructions on package, till done al dente. Drain noodles and rinse them under cold tap water.
2. In small-sized bowl, whisk 2 tablespoons of sesame oil, honey, Sriracha, lime juice, garlic and soy sauce together. Whisk in the corn starch till smooth.
3. Heat the tablespoon of sesame oil in a big wok or pan over medium-high heat. Add the steak & sear for approximately about three to five minutes on each side.
4. Add 2 tablespoons of water, broccoli and mushrooms and stir. cook for approximately about five to six minutes, till tender. Add the sauce and simmer for three minutes.
5. Reduce the heat level to low. Add the cooked noodles. Toss till warmed through and coated fully. Serve with the wedge-cut limes.

Recipe 18: Caramelized Pork Belly

Serving Size: 6

Preparation Time: 20 minutes

Cooking Time: 1 hour 20 minutes

Ingredients:

- 3 tablespoons of fish sauce
- ground black pepper to taste
- 900 grams of pork belly, cut to size
- 2 tablespoons of white sugar
- 5 sliced shallots
- 3 cloves of garlic, chopped
- 380 ml coconut water
- 6 hard-boiled, peeled eggs

Directions:

1. Cut the pork belly into pieces, each containing a layer of meat, fat, and skin.
2. Heat a saucepan or large wok with sugar over medium-high heat for approximately about 5 minutes or until sugar has caramelized into a light brown syrup. Add the prepared pork and turn the heat up to high.
3. Stir-fry the pork for approximately about 3-5 minutes to burn off some of the fat. Add the black pepper and fish sauce and mix well to evenly coat the pork.
4. Stir in the coconut water and let it boil. Add the eggs, turn the heat to low, and let the pork mixture simmer until the pork is tender, about an hour.
5. Take the wok off the stove and keep it warm for approximately about 10 minutes. Remove the prepared fat from the surface of the dish and serve.

Recipe 19: Carrot Peas Papaya Curry

Serving Size: 2

Preparation Time: 15 minutes

Cooking Time: 20 minutes

Ingredients:

- 2 cups of water
- 2 green chilies
- 1 cup of diced raw papaya
- 1 cup of diced carrot
- 1 teaspoon of red chili powder
- ½ cup of peas
- 1 tablespoon of mustard oil
- Salt to taste
- Fresh coriander, chopped, to serve
- 1 teaspoon of cumin
- 1 teaspoon of coriander powder

Directions:

1. Prepare the veggies and wash them properly.
2. In a wok, heat the oil. Fry the onion for approximately about 1 minute.
3. Add the veggies and stir for approximately about 2 minutes.
4. Add the cumin, salt, red chili powder, and coriander powder.
5. Toss for approximately about 5 minutes. Add the chilies, water and cover.
6. Cook on high heat for approximately about 10 minutes. Serve hot with fresh coriander on top.

Recipe 20: Cashew Chicken

Serving Size: 4

Preparation Time: 10 minutes

Cooking Time: 10 minutes

Ingredients:

- 2 tablespoons of honey
- 1 tablespoon of toasted sesame oil
- 2 tablespoons of vegetable oil
- 3 garlic cloves, crushed and chopped
- 1 medium carrot, roll-cut into ½-inch pieces
- 1 red bell pepper, diced into ½-inch pieces
- 1 cup of dry-roasted cashews
- 1 medium onion, halved and cut into ½-inch slices
- 1 cup of chopped bok choy (about ½-inch pieces)
- 4 tablespoons of soy sauce
- 1 teaspoon of cornstarch
- 1 tablespoon of crushed and chopped fresh ginger
- 1 bunch of scallions, cut into ½-inch pieces
- 1 pound of boneless chicken thighs, cut into 1-inch cubes
- Steamed rice, for serving

Directions:

1. In the wok, heat the vegetable oil over high heat until it shimmers.
2. Add the garlic, ginger, and carrot and stir-fry for approximately about a minute. Add the chicken and onion and stir-fry for approximately about a minute. Add the bell pepper and cashews and stir-fry for approximately about a minute. Add the bok choy and stir-fry for approximately about 1 minute.
3. In a prepared medium bowl, whisk together the soy sauce, honey, sesame oil, and cornstarch. Add the prepared sauce to the wok and stir for approximately about 2 minutes, until a glaze forms.
4. Remove from the actual heat and stir in the scallions.
5. Serve over steamed rice.

Recipe 21: Cashew Chicken Stir-Fry

Serving Size: 4

Preparation Time: 25 minutes

Cooking Time: 15 minutes

Ingredients:

- 1 tablespoon of cornstarch
- ½ cup of cashews
- ½ teaspoon of Cajun seasoning
- 1 ¼ cups of chicken broth
- 2 cups of shredded cabbage
- 3 stalks of celery, chopped
- 10 spears of fresh asparagus, trimmed & cut into bite-size pieces
- ½ red bell pepper, sliced into thin strips
- 2 tablespoons of olive oil, divided
- 2 green onions, chopped
- 1 pinch of paprika, or to taste
- 25 sugar snap peas, chopped
- 1 (8-ounce) can of sliced bamboo shoots, drained
- 4 teaspoons of low-sodium soy sauce, divided

Directions:

1. Sprinkle your chicken pieces with Cajun seasoning.
2. Whisk your 3 teaspoons of soy sauce, cornstarch and chicken broth in a bowl.
3. In a wok, heat 1 tablespoon of olive oil over high heat. Cook and stir chicken in prepared hot oil until cooked through or for approximately about 10 minutes. Remove your chicken from wok and drain any liquids.
4. Heat your remaining 1 tablespoon of olive oil in wok over high heat. Stir in the cabbage, asparagus, snow peas, red bell pepper, green onions, bamboo shoots and celery for approximately about 1 minute. Stir in 1 teaspoon of soy sauce. Continue to cook until your veggies are tender, this should take approximately about 3 minutes.
5. Stir in your chicken to the cabbage mixture. Pour your chicken broth over chicken mixture, then reduce heat to simmer until the sauce thickens. Reduce heat to low, add your cashews and cook until heated through. Sprinkle with your paprika, then serve and enjoy!

Recipe 22: Cauliflower Curry

Serving Size: 2

Preparation Time: 15 minutes

Cooking Time: 30 minutes

Ingredients:

- 2 onions, chopped
- Fresh coriander, chopped
- Salt and pepper to taste
- ½ teaspoon of turmeric
- 2 tomatoes, chopped
- 1 red chili, cut in half
- 1 cup of vegetable stock
- 1 tablespoon of cashew paste
- 2 cups of cauliflower florets, cut into big chunks
- 1 tablespoon of butter
- 1 teaspoon of ginger paste
- 1 teaspoon of garlic paste
- 1 tablespoon of tomato sauce

Directions:

1. In a wok, melt the butter. Toss the cauliflower until they get a golden color.
2. Transfer them onto a plate. In the wok add the onion. Toss for approximately about 1 minute.
3. Add the ginger paste, garlic paste, tomato sauce, turmeric, cashew paste and toss for about approximately 2 minutes.
4. Add the chopped tomatoes, salt, pepper, and cook for approximately about 2 minutes.
5. Add the stock and being it to boil. Add the cauliflower florets, red chili and cook for approximately about 10 minutes.
6. Add the coriander and serve hot with rice or tortilla.

Recipe 23: Chicken and Prawn Chow Mein

Serving Size: 4

Preparation Time: 15 minutes

Cooking Time: 35 minutes

Ingredients:

- 1 teaspoon of salt
- 1 teaspoon of vegetable oil
- 1 package of egg noodles
- 2 tablespoons of vegetable oil
- 1 tablespoon of minced garlic
- 1 cup of chopped green cabbage
- 1 cup of chopped carrots
- 1 cup of chopped zucchini
- 1 cup of chopped fresh mushrooms
- 1 cup of chopped broccoli
- 2/3 pounds of prawns, peeled and deveined
- 10 ounces of diced boneless chicken
- 2 tablespoons of chicken bouillon granules
- 3 tablespoons of soy sauce
- 2 teaspoons of salt
- 1/4 teaspoon of sesame oil, to taste
- 1 pinch of white sugar, or to taste

Directions:

2. Boil water in a big cooking pan then add 1 teaspoon of vegetable oil and 1 teaspoon of salt. Toss in the cabbage, prawns, carrots, mushrooms, zucchini, egg noodles, and broccoli and cook for approximately about 5 minutes until they're tender. Wash off under cold water then drain thoroughly.
3. Pour 2 tablespoons of vegetable oil in a big cooking pan or wok and cook the garlic in it for 1 minute while stirring, until aromatic. Mix in the chicken and cook for approximately about 3-4 minutes while stirring until it's browned. Mix in the vegetables, egg noodles, and prawns and cook them for approximately about 2-3 minutes while stirring until they're heated through.
4. Add 2 tablespoons of salt, soy sauce, and chicken bouillon granules to season the mixture and mix thoroughly. Dribble on sesame oil and drizzle with sugar on top of the chow mein just before serving.

Recipe 24: Chicken Hot Pot

Serving Size: 6

Preparation Time: 15 minutes

Cooking Time: 40 minutes

Ingredients:

- 2 tablespoons of cooking oil
- 2 whole star anise pods
- 2 cups of water
- 1 tablespoon of dark soy sauce
- 2 (1-inch) pieces of fresh ginger, sliced diagonally
- 4 (1-inch) pieces of cassia bark or cinnamon bark
- 3 black cardamom pods or 2 white pods and 1 black pod
- 1 pound of boneless, skinless chicken thighs, 1- to 2-inch pieces
- 3 to 7 spicy green chiles, sliced diagonally
- 2 teaspoons of sea salt
- 1 ½ teaspoons of Shaoxing cooking wine or dry sherry

Directions:

1. In a pot of boiling water, parboil the chicken for approximatley about 5 minutes. Drain in a colander and rinse off any residue.
2. In the wok, heat the oil over high heat until it shimmers. Add the ginger and chicken and stir-fry until the chicken is browned, about 5 minutes.
3. Add the cassia bark, cardamom, and star anise. Stir-fry for approximately about another 1 to 2 minutes, until fragrant.
4. Add the dark soy sauce, salt, and wine, and stir-fry for approximatley about minute more to mix well.
5. Add the water and slowly bring to a simmer. Add as many or as actually few chiles as you want for spiciness. Simmer for approximately about 20 to 25 minutes, until the flavors meld. Serve hot.

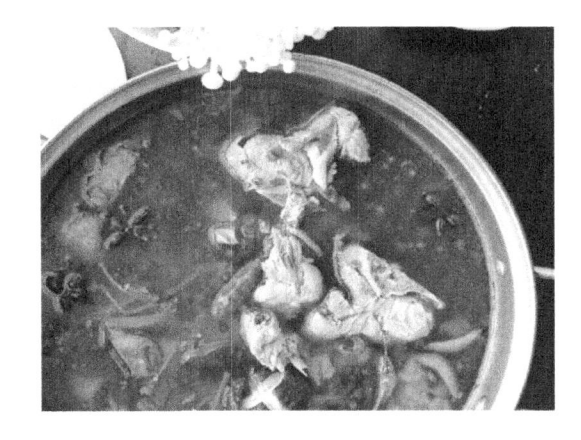

Recipe 25: Chicken Lettuce Wraps

Serving Size: 4

Preparation Time: 15 minutes

Cooking Time: 20 minutes

Ingredients:

- 1 teaspoon of extra virgin olive oil
- 1 onion, white and chopped
- ¼ cup of hoisin sauce
- 1 pound of chicken, lean and ground
- 2 cloves of garlic, minced
- 1 tablespoon of vinegar, rice wine
- 1, 8 ounce can of water chestnuts, thinly sliced and drained
- 1 tablespoon of ginger, grated
- 1 teaspoon of sriracha
- 2 green onions, fresh and sliced
- Dash of salt and black pepper
- 1 head of lettuce, butter and fresh

Directions:

1. Place a large wok over medium to high heat. Add in the olive oil and once the oil begins to smoke add in the ground chicken. cook for approximately about 8 to 10 minutes or until browned. Drain any excess fat.
2. Add in the minced garlic, chopped white onion, hoisin sauce, soy sauce, vinegar, grated ginger and sriracha sauce. Stir well to mix and cook for approximately about 1 to 2 minutes or until the onion is translucent.
3. Season the mixture with a dash of salt and black pepper.
4. Spoon a few spoonfuls of the chicken mixture into the center of a lettuce leaf. Roll and repeat with the remaining chicken mixture and lettuce leaves. Serve immediately.

Recipe 26: Chicken Stir Fry Noodles

Serving Size: 4

Preparation Time: 20 minutes

Cooking Time: 30 minutes

Ingredients:

- 12 ounces of rice noodles
- 3 tablespoons of vegetable oil
- 2 tablespoons of soy sauce
- 2 tablespoons of ketchup
- 1 red bell pepper, thinly sliced
- 1 cup of broccoli, fresh and chopped
- 4 ounces of mushrooms, shiitake or Portobello and thinly sliced
- 1 tablespoon of ginger, fresh, peeled and shredded
- ½ cup of chicken broth
- 1 teaspoon of cornstarch
- 2 chicken breasts, skinless, boneless and cut into small strips
- Touch of sesame oil

Directions:

1. Place a large pot over medium to high heat. Fill with salted water and once boiling add in the noodles. cook for approximately about 5 minutes or until just tender. Drain the noodles and place into a large bowl. Drizzle a touch of vegetable oil over the top to prevent the noodles from sticking to each other. Set aside for now.
2. Place a large wok over high heat. Add in two spoonfuls of vegetable oil and once the oil begins to smoke add in the chicken. cook for approximately about 3 minutes. After this time remove and set the chicken aside.
3. Add the chopped bell pepper, chopped broccoli and mushrooms into the wok. Stir well to mix and cook for approximately about 1 minute. Then add in the shredded ginger. Continue stirring well and cook for approximately about a further 2 minutes.
4. In a large bowl add in the chicken stock, soy sauce, cornstarch and ketchup. Stir well to mix.
5. Add the cooked chicken and noodles into the wok. Toss well to mix. Then pour the sauce mixture over the top and toss to coat. cook for approximately about 3 minutes or until the chicken is fully cooked through. Remove from heat and serve.

Recipe 27: Chili-Garlic Tofu Puffs and Mixed Vegetables

Serving Size: 3

Preparation Time: 10 minutes

Cooking Time: 15 minutes

Ingredients:

- 3 cups of bite-size broccoli florets
- 1 tablespoon of cornstarch
- ⅔ cup of water
- 10 white mushrooms, halved
- 6 garlic cloves, minced
- 1 ¼ teaspoons of sea salt
- 2 tablespoons of canola oil, divided
- 1 small carrot, thinly sliced
- ½ red bell pepper, cut into 1-inch squares
- 4 Tofu Puffs or store-bought tofu puffs, halved
- 1 tablespoon of Shaoxing wine
- 1 teaspoon of granulated sugar
- 1 tablespoon of Sichuan Chili Oil or store-bought chili oil

Directions:

1. Over a temperature of high heat, bring a large saucepan of water to a boil. Add the broccoli and cook it for approximatley about 1 minute, then drain the broccoli in a colander.
2. In a small-sized bowl, mix the cornstarch and water to make a thickener and set it aside.
3. In a large-sized wok or skillet, heat 1 tablespoon of oil over high heat. Add the carrot, bell pepper, and mushroom and stir for approximately about 1 minute. Stir in the last 1 tablespoon of oil, the garlic, and the tofu puffs for approximatley about 1 minute. Add the wine, salt, sugar, and chili oil and stir to combine.
4. 2 minutes after adding the broccoli to the pan, mix it in. Add the cornstarch mixture and stir for approximately about 1 minute, or until the sauce thickens. Serve hot.

Recipe 28: Citrus Carp

Serving Size: 12

Preparation Time: 25 minutes

Cooking Time: 1 hour

Ingredients:

- 1/2 peel of small mandarin orange
- 3 pounds of whole carp, cleaned and scaled
- 3 tablespoons of dry sherry
- 1 tablespoon of black bean sauce
- 2 teaspoons of salt
- 1/4 cup of cornstarch
- 3 tablespoons of minced fresh ginger root
- 1/4 cup of chopped green onion
- 2 tablespoons of soy sauce
- 2 cups of sesame oil
- 2 1/2 tablespoons of chopped
- 1 tablespoon of white sugar
- 6 tablespoons of chicken stock

Directions:

1. Place the orange peel in warm water and allow it to soak until it's soft for approximately about 20 minutes. Drain the peel and wash it off under running water. Squeeze out any excess liquid from the peel then chop it and put it aside.
2. Cut 3-4 slits on one side of the fish then rub salt all over it. Drizzle cornstarch on each sides of the fish.
3. In a meidum-sized wok or pan, heat the oil and then deep fry the fish for approximately about 4-6 minutes per side until each side has browned. Take the fish out of the pan and place it on paper towels to drain.
4. Set aside all the oil, leaving only 2 tablespoons of in the wok or pan. Heat the oil to high heat then add in the garlic, orange peel, green onions, and ginger and stir-fry them in the oil for approximatley about 30 seconds. Pour in the chicken stock, sherry, soy, sauce, bean sauce, and sugar. Blend them together then add the fish. Cover the pan and leave it to allow it to cook for approximately about 8 minutes then serve it right away.

Recipe 29: Classic Mongolian Beef

Serving Size: 4

Preparation Time: 30 minutes

Cooking Time: 1 hour 25 minutes

Ingredients:

- 1 teaspoon of vegetable oil
- 1 teaspoon of soy sauce
- 1 tablespoon of cornstarch
- 1 tablespoon of + ¼ cup of cornstarch
- 2 cloves of garlic, chopped
- 1/3 cup of vegetable oil, for frying
- ½ teaspoon of ginger, minced
- 5 red chili peppers, dried and optional
- ¼ cup of soy sauce, low in sodium
- ¼ cup of chicken broth, low in sodium
- 2 tablespoons of brown sugar, light and packed
- 8 ounces of flank steak, sliced into ¼ inch slices
- 1 tablespoon of water
- 2 scallions, sliced thinly

Directions:

1. In a large bowl add in the beef slices, the vegetable oil, soy sauce and one tablespoon of the cornstarch. Stir well to mix.
2. Dredge the beef in the remaining ¼ cup of the cornstarch until coated on all sides.
3. Place a large wok over high heat. Add in 1/3 cup of the vegetable oil into it. Once the oil begins to smoke add in the beef slices. Sear for approximatley about 1 minute on each side. Transfer to a baking sheet.
4. Drain the oil from the wok, leaving only a spoonful of it. Increase the heat to high. Add in the minced ginger and the chili peppers. Stir well to combine ingredients. cook for approximately about 30 seconds before adding in the minced garlic. Continue to cook for approximately about an additional 10 seconds before adding in the soy sauce and chicken stock. Stir well to mix.
5. Bring this mixture to a simmer and add in the light brown sugar. Stir well until the brown sugar dissolves.
6. Allow to simmer for approximatley about 2 minutes. Add in the remaining spoonful of cornstarch and water into a small bowl. Whisk until smooth in consistency. Add into the wok and stir well to mix. Add the beef back into the wok. Toss to mix.
7. Add in the sliced scallions. Stir well, until fully incorporated into the mix.
8. Remove from heat and serve immediately.

Recipe 30: Coconut Curry Cabbage

Serving Size: 8

Preparation Time: 20 minutes

Cooking Time: 50 minutes

Ingredients:

- 1 tablespoon of olive oil
- 1 clove garlic, minced
- 1 small head cabbage, sliced
- 2 tablespoons of butter
- 1 small yellow onion, thinly sliced
- 3/4 cup of coconut milk
- salt and pepper to taste
- 1 cup of julienned carrots
- 1/2 cups of fresh shredded coconut
- 1/4 cup of chopped green onions
- 2 tablespoons of Indian curry powder
- 1/4 cup of diced fresh tomato
- 1/4 cup of chopped cilantro

Directions:

1. Set the wok or the big skillet on high heat. Heat butter and oil till becoming smoking. Stir-fry garlic, carrot and onion roughly 60 seconds or till onion starts to become tender. Put in curry powder, coconut and cabbage; stir-fry for approximatley about two minutes longer.
2. Lower the heat to a heat of medium low; add in coconut milk, and use pepper and salt to season to taste. Keep covered, and cook to the doneness that you want. To serve, Sprinkle on the cilantro, green onions and tomato.

Recipe 31: Coconut Curry Shrimp

Serving Size: 3

Preparation Time: 10 minutes

Cooking Time: 20 minutes

Ingredients:

- 1 tablespoon of fish sauce
- ¼ teaspoon of pepper
- ¼ teaspoon of sea salt, fine
- 2/3 cup of coconut milk
- 2 green onions, chopped
- 1 ½ tablespoons of curry powder
- 1 teaspoon of brown sugar
- 1 pound of uncooked large shrimp, peeled & deveined
- ¼ cup of fresh cilantro, minced
- 3 cups of hot cooked Jasmine rice
- lime wedges from 1 lime sliced into wedges
- 1 medium sweet red pepper, finely chopped

Directions:

1. In a mixing bowl, combine sea salt, pepper, curry powder, coconut milk, brown sugar and fish sauce. In a large wok, stir-fry your shrimp in 2 tablespoons of coconut milk mixture till shrimp turns pink. Remove from wok and then keep warm.
2. Add your onions, red pepper and the remaining of coconut milk mixture to wok. Bring to a boil, stir and cook for approximately about 4 minutes or until veggies are crisp-tender.
3. Add your shrimp and cilantro to wok and heat through. Serve on a bed of hot Jasmine rice with lime wedges and enjoy!

Recipe 32: Coconut Shrimp

Serving Size: 4

Preparation Time: 10 minutes

Cooking Time: 10 minutes

Ingredients:

- 1 pound of shrimps
- ¼ teaspoon of garlic powder
- 1 teaspoon of cornstarch
- ¼ teaspoon of baking powder
- ¼ cup of all-purpose flour
- ¼ teaspoon of salt
- ¼ teaspoon of baking soda
- ½ cup of coconut flakes
- ¼ teaspoon of onion powder
- ¼ cup of ice water
- Peanut oil for frying

Directions:

1. Whisk the flour, cornstarch, baking powder, baking soda, salt, garlic powder, and onion powder in a bowl.
2. Dredge the shrimp in the flour mixture before dipping them in the water.
3. Coat the shrimp with coconut flakes. Deep the fry the shrimp in a suitable wok filled with oil at 350 degrees F, until golden brown.
4. Place the shrimp on a platter that has been lined with a paper towel. Serve warm.

Recipe 33: Crispy French Fries

Serving Size: 4

Preparation Time: 15 minutes

Cooking Time: 40 minutes

Ingredients:

- 2 tablespoons of distilled white vinegar
- 2 quarts of peanut oil
- Kosher salt, as required, to taste
- 2 pounds russet potatoes, peeled, cleaned & cut into ¼ by ¼" fries

Directions:

1. Add 2 quarts of water with the vinegar and 2 tablespoons of salt in a large saucepan, bring it to a boil. Once done, carefully add the potatoes and continue to cook for approximately about 8 to 10 minutes. Drain & spread on a large-sized rimmed baking sheet lined with paper towel. Let dry for a couple of minutes.
2. In the meantime, heat the oil until hot over high heat in a large wok or Dutch oven. Work in batches and add approximately ¼ of the fries carefully into the hot oil. Cook roughly for approximatley about a minute, stirring & dipping the fries occasionally using a wire mesh spider. Once done, transfer them to a separate baking sheet lined with paper towel. Repeat this cooking step with the leftover potatoes until all of the fries have cooked through. Let the potatoes to cool down to room temperature.
3. Heat the oil again over high heat until hot. Fry half of fries for approximatley about 3 to 4 minutes, until turn light golden brown & crisp. Place them into a bowl lined with the paper towels to drain & season with the kosher salt. Serve immediately and enjoy.

Recipe 34: Crispy Steamed Duck

Serving Size: 4

Preparation Time: 10 minutes

Cooking Time: 20 minutes

Ingredients:

- 4 boneless, skin-on duck breasts
- 2 tablespoons of cornstarch
- 5 scallions, sliced
- Hoisin sauce, for dipping
- Steamed rice, noodles, or pancakes, for serving
- 1 tablespoon of Chinese five-spice powder

Directions:

1. Score the duck skin with shallow crosscuts about ¼ inch apart.
2. Place the wok or a pot fitted with a steamer basket over high heat. Add water until it is 1 inch below the bottom of the basket. When the water boils, immediately place the duck, skin-side down, in the basket, cover, and steam for approximatley about 10 minutes, or until the water is almost gone. Remove the duck and steamer basket, but leave the remaining liquid.
3. Reduce the heat to medium for approximately about 3 minutes more to evaporate the remaining water, leaving just the duck fat.
4. Transfer the duck to a large zip-top bag with the cornstarch and five-spice powder. Massage for approximatley about 2 minutes.
5. Heat the duck fat over medium-high heat until it shimmers. Add the coated duck, skin-side up, and fry for 1 minute. Flip the duck over and fry for approximatley about 2 minutes, or until the skin is crispy brown.
6. Thinly slice the duck or cut it into cubes, sprinkle it with scallions, and serve with steamed rice, noodles, or pancakes, and hoisin sauce for dipping.

Recipe 35: Curried Chicken Wings

Serving Size: 4

Preparation Time: 25 minutes

Cooking Time: 55 minutes

Ingredients:

- ¼ cup of peanut oil, divided
- 1 pound of chicken wings
- ¼ cup of red curry paste
- 1 piece of leek, trimmed and thinly sliced
- 2 tablespoons of fresh basil leaves, chopped
- 1-13.5 ounces of coconut milk
- 1 pound of winter squash, seeded, and cubed
- 15 ounces of chickpeas, drained and rinsed
- ½ cup of chicken stock

Directions:

1. Heat a tablespoon of peanut oil in a wok on high heat and brown chicken wings for approximately about 3 minutes per batch, flipping once. Remove with a slotted spoon to a bowl and set aside.
2. In the same wok, heat the remaining oil and cook the leeks until they are softened.
3. Stir in curry paste and let it cook for approximately about a minute.
4. Put back chicken wings, plus squash. Pour in coconut milk and water.
5. Simmer for approximately about 20 minutes, covered.
6. Remove the lid, stir in chickpeas, and let cook for approximately about another 10 minutes.
7. Garnish with freshly chopped basil leaves.

Recipe 36: Deep-Fried Salmon and Miso Wontons

Serving Size: 40

Preparation Time: 40 minutes

Cooking Time: 15 minutes

Ingredients:

- 1 (8-ounce) skinless salmon fillet
- 1 tablespoon of soy sauce
- 1 tablespoon of white or yellow miso
- 1 teaspoon of toasted sesame oil
- 1 (12-ounce) package square wonton wrappers
- 2 fresh garlic cloves, crushed and chopped
- 2 cups of oil, for deep-frying

Directions:

1. In a food processor, combine and pulse the salmon, miso, garlic, sesame oil, and soy sauce.
2. To make the wontons, place a wonton wrapper on a work surface so it looks like a baseball diamond with you sitting behind home plate.
3. Fill a small bowl with water. Using a clean fingertip, paint around the baselines with the water.
4. Place a teaspoon of the filling in the center, where the pitcher's mound would be.
5. Bring home plate up to second base, folding the wrapper into a triangle, thereby enclosing the filling. Seal the edges.
6. In the wok, heat the oil to 350°F, or until a wooden chopstick dipped into the oil causes bubbles.
7. Deep-fry the wontons until golden brown color develops on both sides, flipping as needed.
8. Serve with your favorite dipping sauce.

Recipe 37: Dry-Fried Cauliflower

Serving Size: 4

Preparation Time: 20 minutes

Cooking Time: 15 minutes

Ingredients:

- 1 medium head cauliflower
- 1 scallion
- 3 garlic cloves, sliced
- ¾ teaspoon of sea salt
- 2 fresh bird's eye chilies, sliced into thin rings
- 2 tablespoons of Chinese light soy sauce
- 1 tablespoon of canola oil, plus more for deep-frying
- ¾ teaspoon of granulated sugar

Directions:

1. Cut the cauliflower florets into bite-size pieces and then cut the stems into pieces of about the same size. Halve the scallion lengthwise, then cut it crosswise into 1-inch segments.
2. In a large-sized deep pot, heat at least 3 inches of oil over high heat. When the cooking oil is very hot and begins to smoke (425°F), lower the cauliflower into the oil all in one batch and deep-fry for approximatley about 30 seconds, or until it is lightly golden. Remove the cauliflower using a spider sieve or a slotted spoon.
3. In a wok or large-sized skillet, heat 1 tablespoon of oil over high heat. Add the scallion, garlic, and chilies and stir until fragrant.
4. Add the cauliflower to the wok and stir for approximately about 1 minute. Add the soy sauce, salt, and sugar and stir for approximately about another minute to thoroughly combine everything. Remove the pan from the heat. Serve hot.

Recipe 38: Egg Curry in Coconut Milk

Serving Size: 4

Preparation Time: 20 minutes

Cooking Time: 50 minutes

Ingredients:

- 1 black cardamom
- 1 ½ teaspoons of red chili powder
- 1 teaspoon of dried fenugreek leaves
- 1 bay leaf
- 4 large whole eggs, hard-boiled
- 1 tablespoon of garlic, paste
- 1 tablespoon of ginger, paste
- 4 green chilies, minced
- ½ teaspoon of turmeric powder
- 1 tablespoon of coriander powder
- 4 whole black peppercorns
- 3 onions, paste
- 1 cup of coconut milk
- 2 tomatoes, pureed
- 1 teaspoon of cumin powder
- 2 cardamom pods or seeds
- Salt according to taste
- 1" cinnamon stick
- Oil, as required
- 1 tablespoon of coriander leaves, finely chopped

Directions:

1. Peel the boiled eggs & coat with a bit of turmeric powder; set them aside.
2. Next, over moderate heat in a large frying pan; heat 4 tablespoons of oil until hot & fry the coated eggs until they turn golden, for a couple of minutes. Transfer the fried eggs to a large plate; set aside.
3. Next, over moderate heat in a wok; heat the oil until hot.
4. Add in the bay leaf & whole spices; continue to cook until crackled, for approximatley about a couple of minutes.
5. Now add in the onion followed by ginger and garlic paste; fry the ingredients until brown, for a couple of minutes.
6. Add in the minced green chilies followed by tomato puree; give the ingredients a good stir and continue frying for approximately about a couple of more minutes.
7. Immediately add the coriander powder, red chili powder, and cumin powder; continue to mix the ingredients until incorporated well.
8. Fry the mix for approximately about couple of minutes until the oil just begins leaving the sides.
9. Add approximately ½ cup of water & mix well. Taste and adjust the prepared amount of salt, if required.
10. Cover & cook for approximately about 5 more minutes.
11. Remove the lid & immediately pour the coconut milk; stir well and remove it from the heat.
12. Carefully add the fried eggs & sprinkle with a bit of coriander. Serve hot and enjoy.

Recipe 39: Egg Drop Soup

Serving Size: 6

Preparation Time: 10 minutes

Cooking Time: 10 minutes

Ingredients:

- 8 ½ cups of vegetable broth, divided
- 4 large eggs, beaten
- ¼ cup of cornstarch
- 1 ounce of dried, sliced shiitake or tree ear mushrooms
- 4 scallions, both white and green parts, cut into ¼-inch pieces

Directions:

1. In the wok, combine 8 cups of broth and the mushrooms. Bring to a boil.
2. In a small bowl, create a slurry with ¼ cup of cornstarch and the remaining ½ cup of broth.
3. Stir the prepared cornstarch slurry into the boiling broth until the broth thickens and clarifies. You can add more or less of the slurry for thicker or thinner soup.
4. Stir the broth gently in one direction while drizzling the beaten eggs into the wok. Cook for approximately about 1 minute, until strands and billows of poached egg form.
5. Garnish with the scallions, bruising them by squeezing them while dropping them into the broth. Serve immediately.

Recipe 40: Fiery Pepper Chicken

Serving Size: 4

Preparation Time: 20 minutes

Cooking Time: 35 minutes

Ingredients:

- 2 teaspoons of soy sauce
- 1/2 teaspoon of salt
- 1/4 cup of cornstarch, or as needed
- 3 cups of peanut oil for frying
- 4 cloves garlic, minced
- 1 tablespoon of minced fresh ginger root
- 2 green onions, julienned
- 2 long, green chilies - cut into 1/2-inch pieces
- 1 teaspoon of Chinese cooking wine
- 2 cups of dried chilies, chopped
- 2 tablespoons of Szechuan peppercorns
- 2 teaspoons of Chinese cooking wine
- 1/2 pound of boneless chicken, 1/2 inch cubes
- 1/2 teaspoon of white sugar
- 1/2 teaspoon of salt

Directions:

1. Combine 1/2 teaspoon of salt and 1 teaspoon of cooking wine in a bowl and stir them together. Add the chicken and coat it by stirring it in. Leave it to marinate for approximatley about 2-3 minutes. Combine the marinated chicken and cornstarch in a big sealable plastic bag then shake it to coat the chicken.
2. In a big cooking pan or wok, heat the peanut oil on high heat. Fry the chicken for approximatley about 7-10 minutes in the oil until the edges start to get crisp. To drain the chicken, place it on a platter lined with paper towels. Discard the oil, leaving 2 tablespoons.
3. Reheat the remaining 2 tablespoons of oil in the medium-sized wok on medium-high heat. Cook the garlic, green onions and ginger in the oil for a minute until fragrant. Add the green chilies, Szechuan peppercorns, and crushed dried chilies then continue to fry for approximatley about another 20 seconds. Put the chicken cubes back to the wok and add 2 teaspoons of cooking wine, soy sauce, 1/2 teaspoon of salt, and sugar while stirring until they are well blended together. Turn the heat and off serve right away.

Recipe 41: Fried Brown Rice

Serving Size: 4

Preparation Time: 5 minutes

Cooking Time: 10 minutes

Ingredients:

- 1/2 onion (chopped)
- 2 tablespoons of butter
- 3 cups of cooked brown rice
- 2 large eggs
- 1 cup of diced, well cooked ham
- 3 tablespoons of peanut oil, divided, or more as needed
- salt and pepper to taste
- 1/2 cups of shredded cheddar cheese

Directions:

1. Heat a prepared wok or frying pan over high heat for approximatley about 1 minute. Thoroughly add 2 tablespoons of peanut oil to the wok and reduce the heat to a heat of medium. Cook the onion and stir until it starts to soften, approximately about 3 minutes.
2. Beat the eggs directly into the wok. Stir the ham into the wok and cook just until the eggs start to set but are still runny. Stir the ham into the wok, approximately about 1 1/2 minutes, and cook just until heated through.
3. Stir butter and remaining 1 tablespoon of peanut oil into wok for approximatley about 1 minute; Allow to heat up for 10 seconds. Add rice and cook, stirring constantly, for approximatley about 3 to 4 minutes when rice starts to stick; season fried rice with salt and pepper; Scatter cheddar cheese on top.

Recipe 42: Fried Mushrooms with Baby Corn

Serving Size: 4

Preparation Time: 10 minutes

Cooking Time: 15 minutes

Ingredients:

- 2 tablespoons of cooking oil
- 3 cloves of garlic, chopped
- 1 tablespoon of oyster sauce
- 2 teaspoons of cornstarch
- 3 tablespoons of water
- 1 onion, diced 8 sliced baby corns
- 350 grams of fresh mushrooms, sliced
- 1 tablespoon of fish sauce
- 1 tablespoon of light soy sauce
- 1 sliced red chilli
- 1/4 cup of chopped fresh cilantro

Directions:

1. Heat the oil in a prepared large skillet or wok over medium-high heat; let the garlic brown in the hot oil for approximately about 5 to 7 minutes.
2. Add the onion and corn and cook until onion is translucent, approximatley about 5 to 7 minutes. Add the mushrooms and cook until slightly soft, approximately about 2 minutes.
3. Whisk together the prepared cornstarch and water in a small bowl until the cornstarch is actually dissolved in the water; pour them into the mushroom mixture. Cook and stir until the mixture thickens and is glossy.
4. Arrange on a serving plate; Garnish with the chilli and coriander to serve.

Recipe 43: Fried Pork Chops with Onion

Serving Size: 4

Preparation Time: 20 minutes

Cooking Time: 15 minutes

Ingredients:

- 4 boneless pork loin chops
- 1 tablespoon of Shaoxing wine
- 2 tablespoons of light soy sauce
- 1 teaspoon of dark soy sauce
- ½ teaspoon of freshly ground black pepper
- Kosher salt
- 3 cups of vegetable oil
- 2 tablespoons of cornstarch
- 3 peeled fresh ginger slices, each about the size of a quarter
- 1 medium yellow onion, thinly sliced
- 2 garlic cloves, finely minced
- ½ teaspoon of red wine vinegar
- Sugar

Directions:

1. Pound the pork chops with a meat mallet until they are ½ inch thick. Place in a bowl and season with the rice wine, pepper, and a small pinch of salt. Marinate for approximatley about 10 minutes.
2. Pour the oil into the wok; the oil should be about 1 to 1½ inches deep. Bring the oil to 375°F over medium-high heat. You can tell the oil is at the right temperature when you dip the end of a wooden spoon into the oil. If the oil bubbles and sizzles around it, the oil is ready.
3. Working in 2 batches, coat the chops with the cornstarch. Gently lower them one at a time into the oil and fry for approximatley about 5 to 6 minutes, until golden. Transfer to a paper towel–lined plate.
4. Pour out all but 1 tablespoon of prepared oil from the wok and set it over medium-high heat. Season the oil by adding the ginger and a pinch of salt. Allow the ginger to sizzle in the oil for approximately about 30 seconds, swirling gently.
5. Stir-fry the onion for approximately about 4 minutes, until translucent and soft. Add the garlic and stir-fry for approximately about another 30 seconds, or until fragrant. Transfer to the plate with the pork chops.
6. Into the wok, pour the light soy, dark soy, red wine vinegar, and a pinch of sugar and stir to combine. Bring to a boil and return the onion and pork chops to the wok. Toss to combine as the sauce begins to thicken slightly. Remove the ginger and discard. Transfer to a platter and serve immediately.

Recipe 44: Garlic Chicken

Serving Size: 4

Preparation Time: 10 minutes

Cooking Time: 5 minutes

Ingredients:

- 2 tablespoons of dark soy sauce
- 2 tablespoons of cooking oil
- 1 tablespoon of chopped, fresh ginger
- 4 scallions, both white and green parts, cut into ¼-inch pieces
- 4 garlic cloves, crushed and chopped
- 1 pound of boneless, skinless chicken thighs, ¼-inch pieces across the grain
- Rice or noodles, for serving

Directions:

1. In a medium bowl, combine the chicken and dark soy sauce.
2. In the wok, heat the oil over medium-high heat until it shimmers.
3. Add the ginger, garlic, and chicken and stir-fry for approximatley about 3 minutes, until browned and fragrant.
4. Add the scallions and stir-fry for approximatley about 1 minute to mix. Serve over rice or noodles.

Recipe 45: Ginger Broccoli

Serving Size: 4

Preparation Time: 15 minutes

Cooking Time: 18 minutes

Ingredients:

- 1 ½ pound of fresh broccoli
- 1 onion, cut into crescents
- 1/2 teaspoon of salt
- 1 tablespoon of rice wine mixed with 1 teaspoon of water
- 3 tablespoons of oil
- 6 slices fresh ginger, finely shredded

Directions:

1. Remove broccoli florets out from the main stem, leaving each with its stalk.
2. Using a sharp paring knife, peel the stiff skin off the stems below the florets. Make bite-sized bits out of the stems.
3. Heat oil on medium fire in a wok, and then add the broccoli and ginger to stir-fry for approximately 1 minute, just until the broccoli has darkened in color. cook for approximately about another minute after adding the onions.
4. Steam the broccoli for approximatley about 1–2 minutes with rice wine and water, covered securely with a lid.
5. Remove cover, whisk in the salt, and transfer the mixture to a serving plate.

Recipe 46: Ginger Golden Chicken Curry

Serving Size: 4

Preparation Time: 15 minutes

Cooking Time: 25 minutes

Ingredients:

- 1 teaspoon of ginger paste
- 2-3 garlic cloves, minced
- ¼ teaspoon of paprika powder
- ½ teaspoon of sea salt
- ¼ teaspoon of curry powder
- 18 ounces of chicken, pieces
- 1 cup of tomato paste
- ¼ cup of fried onion
- 2 tablespoons of coriander leaves, chopped
- ¼ teaspoon of cumin powder
- 1 inch ginger slice, julienned
- 1 cup of water
- 2 tablespoons of butter

Directions:

1. In a wok melt butter and fry chicken until golden.
2. Add in tomato paste, ginger paste, and garlic, stir fry until water is dried out.
3. Seasons with salt, paprika, curry powder, onion, and cumin powder.
4. Now add julienned ginger and water, mix well.
5. Cover and let to prepare for approximatley about 10-15 minutes on medium heat.
6. When chicken is softened, and water is dried sprinkle coriander leaves.
7. Sever hot and enjoy.

Recipe 47: Kale and Bell Pepper Frittata

Serving Size: 3

Preparation Time: 10 minutes

Cooking Time: 17 minutes

Ingredients:

- 6 eggs
- Salt, as required
- ¼ cup of fresh chives, chopped
- 1 tablespoon of olive oil
- ½ teaspoon of ground turmeric
- 1 small red bell pepper, chopped
- 1 cup of fresh kale, trimmed and chopped

Directions:

1. In a bowl, add the eggs and salt and beat well. Set aside.
2. In a cast-iron wok, heat the oil over medium-low heat and sprinkle with turmeric.
3. Immediately stir in the bell pepper and kale and sauté for approximately about 2 minutes.
4. Place the beaten eggs over bell pepper mixture evenly and immediately reduce the heat to low.
5. Cover the wok and cook for approximately about 10-15 minutes.
6. Remove from the actual heat and set aside for approximately about 5 minutes.
7. Cut into equal-sized wedges and serve.

Recipe 48: Kung Pao Chicken

Serving Size: 4

Preparation Time: 25 minutes

Cooking Time: 40 minutes

Ingredients:

- ¼ cup of water
- ½ teaspoon of salt
- ½ of an egg, large
- ¼ cup of cornstarch
- 1 teaspoon of ginger, ground
- 1 teaspoon of garlic, ground
- 1 teaspoon of red chili pepper, crushed
- 2 tablespoons of vegetable oil
- 1 teaspoon of white wine
- 2 ½ tablespoon of soy sauce
- 1/3 cup of water
- 2 ½ tablespoon of vegetable oil, divided
- 1 pound of chicken breasts, boneless, skinless and cut into small pieces
- 12 chili peppers, whole and dried
- ¼ cup of green onions, fresh and sliced
- ½ tablespoon of cornstarch, mixed with ½ tablespoon of water
- 1 teaspoon of sesame oil
- 2 ounces of peanuts, dry and roasted
- 1 red bell pepper, cut into small cubes
- 1 zucchini, cut into small cubes

Directions:

1. In a large bowl add in the chicken, water, dash of salt, half of the egg, ¼ cup of the cornstarch and 2 spoonfuls of vegetable oil. Stir well to mix and cover with foil. Place into the fridge to marinate for approximatley about 1 hour.
2. Use a small bowl and add in the white wine, soy sauce and water. Stir well to mix and set aside.
3. Place a large wok over medium heat. Add in two spoonfuls of vegetable oil. Once the oil begins to smoke and add the chicken to the wok. cook for approximately about 60 seconds over high heat. After this time remove the chicken and set aside.
4. Add another spoonful of prepared oil to the wok. Once it is hot enough add in the chopped red bell pepper and zucchini pieces. Stir well to mix and cook for approximately about 1 to 2 minutes or until caramelized. Remove the vegetables and set aside.
5. Add in the chopped green onions, roasted peanuts, ground ginger, ground garlic, sesame oil and crushed red pepper flakes. Stir well to mix. cook for approximately about a few seconds before adding in the wine mixture.
6. Bring the mixture to a boil. Once boiling add in the cornstarch mixture. cook for approximately about 1 to 2 minutes or until thick in consistency.
7. Add the cooked chicken and vegetables back into the wok. Toss to mix and cook for approximately about an additional minute.
8. Remove from heat and serve immediately.

Recipe 49: Kung Pao Potatoes

Serving Size: 3

Preparation Time: 15 minutes

Cooking Time: 30 minutes

Ingredients:

- 2 tablespoons of black vinegar
- 2 tablespoons of Chinese light soy sauce
- 3 tablespoons of granulated sugar
- ½ teaspoon of sea salt
- 1 tablespoon of dark soy sauce
- 1 scallion, ½-inch lengths
- ⅓ cup of roasted peanuts
- 2 tablespoons of Shaoxing wine
- ¼ teaspoon of ground white pepper
- 1½ teaspoons of cornstarch
- 1 tablespoon of water
- 2 tablespoons of canola oil, plus more for deep-frying
- 3 medium yellow potatoes (1lb / 454g), peeled and cut into ½-inch cubes
- 2 tablespoons of red Sichuan peppercorns
- 6 dried red facing heaven chili peppers, cut into ½-inch segments
- 1 ginger, thinly sliced
- 3 garlic cloves, thinly sliced

Directions:

1. In a small-sized bowl, mix the black vinegar, light soy sauce, dark soy sauce, rice wine, white pepper, sugar, salt, cornstarch, and water. Set aside.
2. In a deep pot, heat 3 inches of oil over medium-high heat. When a wooden chopstick lowered into the oil immediately sizzles (about 350°F), fry the potatoes for approximately about 4 to 5 minutes, until they float. Transfer to a plate with a spider strainer or slotted spoon.
3. In a wok or skillet, heat 2 tablespoons of oil over medium-low heat. Fry the Sichuan peppercorns for 3 to 4 minutes, until they turn dark brown. Remove and discard the peppercorns. Add the chilies to the pan and stir until they darken slightly. Add the ginger, garlic, and scallion to the pan and stir them until fragrant. Add the potatoes and stir for approximately about 1 minute over medium-high heat. Add the sauce and stir for approximately about 40 seconds, or until it thickens. Add the peanuts and stir to mix.

Recipe 50: Lime Fry

Serving Size: 4

Preparation Time: 20 minutes

Cooking Time: 30 minutes

Ingredients:

- 3 tablespoons of lime juice
- 1/2 cups of chopped fresh basil
- 2 tablespoons of peanut oil
- 3 tablespoons of soy sauce
- 2 tablespoons of maple syrup
- 1 tablespoon of minced fresh ginger root
- 1 pound zucchini, diced
- 16 ounces of extra-firm tofu
- 2 tablespoons of red curry paste
- 1 red bell pepper, diced
- 1 (14 ounces) can coconut milk

Directions:

1. In a wok or large-sized skillet, heat the peanut oil over high heat. Put in the tofu and stir-fry until it turns golden brown. Take out the tofu and put aside, reserve the remaining oil in the wok.
2. Toss the ginger and curry paste into the hot oil for a few seconds until the curry paste gets fragrant and the ginger starts to turn golden. Put in bell pepper and the zucchini; cook while stirring for 1 minute. Pour in tofu, coconut milk, maple syrup, soy sauce, and lime juice. Simmer the coconut milk and cook for approximately about a few minutes until the vegetables become tender and the tofu is hot. Right before serving, mix in the chopped basil.

Recipe 51: Lion Head Meatballs

Serving Size: 4

Preparation Time: 20 minutes

Cooking Time: 45 minutes

Ingredients:

- 1 pound of Bok choy
- 1 or 2 minced onions, green
- 1 teaspoon of minced ginger, fresh
- 3 tablespoons of soy sauce, light
- 1/2 teaspoon of oil, Asian sesame
- 3/4 teaspoon of salt, kosher
- 1 egg, large
- 1 pound of ground pork, lean
- 1 teaspoon of granulated sugar
- 2 & 1/2 teaspoon of pale, dry sherry
- Optional: pepper, black
- 2-3 tablespoons of corn starch
- 2 tablespoons of oil, vegetable
- 1 & 1/2 cups of broth, chicken, low sodium

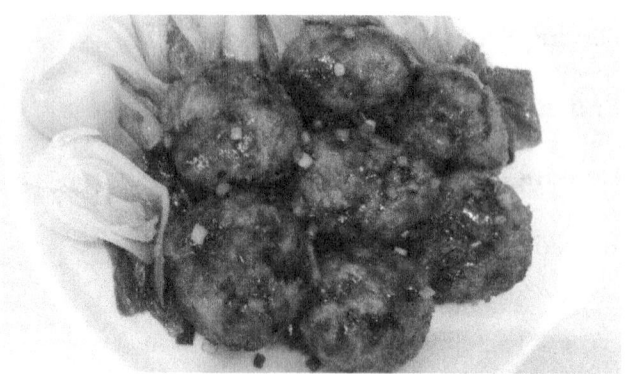

Directions:

1. Wash, then drain Bok choy. Cut it crossways in three-inch strips.
2. Mince green onions and ginger.
3. In small-sized bowl, use a fork to beat egg.
4. In medium mixing bowl, combine pork with ginger, green onions, sugar, salt, sherry, sesame oil, 1 tablespoon of soy sauce, egg and pepper, if you're using it. Use your fingers and mix ingredients well.
5. Add corn starch as is needed so mixture isn't overly wet. Start with 2 tablespoons of and add 1 teaspoon of after another till the consistency is as you desire.
6. Form pork into four large-sized meatballs. Flatten just a bit so they're not fully rounded.
7. Heat 2 tablespoons of oil in wok on med-high. When oil has heated, add the meatballs. Cook till bottoms have browned, five minutes. Cook other side.
8. In large pan, heat broth and 2 tablespoons of soy sauce till boiling.
9. Add meatballs. Lower heat and cover pan. Simmer for 10-12 minutes.
10. Add Bok choy to pan. Laying it on top of meatballs will help it to steam nicely.
11. Simmer for 15 minutes more, till meatballs have no pink in center and have cooked fully through.
12. Lay meatballs individually on small plates with greens surrounding them, along with some broth and Bok choy. Serve.

Recipe 52: Long Life Noodles

Serving Size: 4

Preparation Time: 15 minutes

Cooking Time: 15 minutes

Ingredients:

- 3 quarts of water
- 1 pack of Yi Mein noodles
- 2 teaspoon of soy sauce, dark
- ½ teaspoon of oyster sauce
- ½ teaspoon of sesame oil
- 1/8 teaspoon of sugar
- ¼ teaspoon of salt
- 1 tablespoon of water, hot
- 2 teaspoon of soy sauce
- Dash of white pepper
- 3 to 5 mushrooms, shiitake and sliced thinly
- 3 to 4 tablespoon of canola oil
- 8 ounces of chives, Chinese and cut into small pieces

Directions:

1. Place a large wok over medium to high heat. Add in the three quarts of water. Once the water is actually boiling add in the noodles. Boil for 5 minutes or until soft. Remove, drain the water and set the noodles aside.
2. Use a small bowl and add in the sugar, dash of salt and one spoonful of hot water. Stir well to mix or until the sugar is fully dissolved. Add in the soy sauce, dark soy sauce, oyster sauce, sesame oil and dash of white pepper. Stir well until mixed.
3. In the same wok add in a touch of canola oil. Once the oil begins to smoke add in the mushrooms and chives. cook for approximately about 20 seconds before adding in the cooked noodles. Toss to mix.
4. Pour the sauce mixture over the noodle mixture. Toss to mix and cook for approximately about 1 minute. Add in the remaining canola oil and stir to incorporate.
5. Add in the remaining chives and continue to cook for approximately about 1 to 3 minutes before removing from heat. Serve immediately.

Recipe 53: Lotus Leaf Wraps

Serving Size: 8
Preparation Time: 20 minutes
Cooking Time: 1 hour and 10 minutes

Ingredients:

- 4 pieces of lotus leaves, halved
- ½ pound of pork loin, finely chopped
- 2 tablespoons of Chinese rice wine
- ¼ teaspoon of sesame oil
- 7 ounces of skinless and boneless chicken thighs, cubed
- 1 tablespoon of light soy sauce
- 1 teaspoon of dark soy sauce
- 1 clove of garlic, chopped
- 2 pieces of Chinese sausages, chopped
- 1 ½ teaspoon of cornflour
- 4 Chinese dried black mushrooms, soaked in hot water, drained, and finely chopped
- 7 ounces of sticky rice, soaked in water for 1 hour, drained, and steamed
- ¼ teaspoon of salt
- 2 tablespoons of vegetable oil
- Salt and ground black pepper to taste

Directions:

1. Sprinkle some salt on pork and chicken and mix to coat. Set aside.
2. Heat oil in a wok and stir fry garlic for approximately about a minute.
3. Add pork and chicken and cook for approximately about a few minutes until they are no longer pink.
4. Stir in sausages and mushrooms and cook for approximately about another minute.
5. Meanwhile, mix light and dark soy sauce, plus rice wine in a small bowl.
6. Pour the sauce mixture into the wok and let it simmer.
7. Add cornflour and water mixture and stir fry for 2 minutes more until thickened.
8. Season with salt and pepper and cook for approximately about a further 2 minutes.
9. Turn off fire and fold in sesame oil into the mixture. Set aside to cool down.
10. Boil enough water in a steamer pot over medium fire.
11. Divide the rice and filling into 8.
12. Place each section onto a lotus leaf half, with the rice at the bottom and the meat and veggie mix on top. Bring the edges on top and tie up with a kitchen string.
13. Arrange the lotus wraps in a heatproof dish placed inside a steamer basket. Add on top of the steamer pot. Steam for 15 minutes.
14. Serve immediately.

Recipe 54: Mandarin Pork Stir-Fry

Serving Size: 4

Preparation Time: 10 minutes

Cooking Time: 25 minutes

Ingredients:

- 1 package (14-ounce) frozen sugar snap peas
- ½ teaspoon of ground ginger
- ½ teaspoon of garlic powder
- ½ cup of orange juice
- 2 cups of uncooked instant rice
- 1 can (11-ounce) mandarin oranges, drained
- 1 tablespoon of cornstarch
- 2 tablespoons of soy sauce
- 1 pound of Pork tenderloin, sliced into 2-inch strips
- ¼ cup of water

Directions:

1. Cook your instant rice according to the package directions. In a small bowl, mix your garlic powder, cornstarch and ginger.
2. Stir in the orange juice until smooth. Stir in the soy sauce, water, and set aside.
3. In a large wok, stir-fry pork in oil until the juices run clear. Remove to a platter and keep warm. Add your snow peas to the same wok for a few minutes or until tender. Return your pork to wok and stir in the orange juice mixture.
4. Cook and stir for approximately about 2 minutes or until thickened. Stir in the oranges and serve with rice.

Recipe 55: Mushroom Pepper Steak

Serving Size: 4

Preparation Time: 15 minutes

Cooking Time: 15 minutes

Ingredients:

- 1/8 teaspoon of pepper
- 1 tablespoon of cornstarch
- 1 cup of julienned green pepper
- 2 cups of fresh mushrooms, sliced
- 1 pound of beef top sirloin steak, sliced into thin strips
- ½ cup of low-sodium beef broth
- 6 green onions, sliced
- 1 garlic clove, minced
- 2 medium tomatoes, sliced into wedges
- 3 teaspoons of canola oil, divided
- ½ teaspoon of fresh gingeroot, minced
- 6 tablespoons of low-sodium soy sauce, divided
- hot cooked rice, of your choice (optional)

Directions:

1. In a bowl, combine 3 tablespoons of soy sauce and pepper, then add beef. Turn to coat then cover and place in fridge for approximately about 60 minutes.
2. In a prepared small bowl, combine remaining soy sauce, cornstarch and broth until smooth, then set aside.
3. Next, drain your beef and discard the marinade. In a large wok, stir-fry the ginger and garlic in 2 teaspoons of oil for a minute over medium-high heat.
4. Add the beef to wok and stir-fry for another 6 minutes or until meat is no longer pink. Remove the beef from heat and keep warm.
5. In remaining oil, stir-fry the peppers for 1-minute. Add in your mushrooms and stir-fry for another 2 minutes or until peppers are crisp and tender.
6. Stir your broth mixture then add it to your veggie mixture. Bring to a very hot boil and cook for approximately about 2 minutes or until thickened.
7. Return your beef to wok along with tomatoes and onions. cook for approximately about 2 minutes or until heated through. Serve over a bed of rice and enjoy!

Recipe 56: Orange Peel Beef

Serving Size: 6

Preparation Time: 25 minutes

Cooking Time: 1 hour and 31 minutes

Ingredients:

- 1 1/2 lbs. beef top sirloin, thinly sliced
- 1 tablespoon of low-sodium soy sauce
- 1 tablespoon of cornstarch
- 1 tablespoon of peanut oil
- 3 cloves garlic, minced
- 1 teaspoon of dark sesame oil
- 1/2 teaspoon of baking soda
- 1 tablespoon of rice vinegar
- 1 teaspoon of dark sesame oil
- 1 tablespoon of low-sodium soy sauce
- 1 tablespoon of finely shredded orange zest
- 1 tablespoon of brown sugar
- 1 tablespoon of minced fresh ginger root
- 2 tablespoons of frozen orange juice concentrate, thawed
- 1 teaspoon of cornstarch
- 1/4 teaspoon of red pepper flakes

Directions:

1. In a bowl, mix 1 tablespoon of soy sauce, 1 teaspoon of sesame oil, 1 tablespoon of cornstarch, baking soda and beef until well combined. Refrigerate the bowl for 1-3 hours after covering it.
2. Heat a big non-stick skillet or wok with peanut oil over high heat. Put in the ginger, red pepper flakes, garlic and orange zest and stir-fry for 20-30 seconds until the garlic starts to brown. Put in the marinated beef and stir-fry for approximately about 5 minutes until the beef is crispy and is starting to turn brown in color. In a small bowl, mix orange juice concentrate, rice vinegar, 1 tablespoon of soy sauce, 1 teaspoon of sesame oil, 1 teaspoon of cornstarch and brown sugar. Pour it into the beef mixture and cook for approximately about 30 seconds until the sauce turns clear and is thick in consistency.

Recipe 57: Oyster Mushroom

Serving Size: 3

Preparation Time: 10 minutes

Cooking Time: 10 minutes

Ingredients:

- 1 pound of king oyster mushrooms, sliced
- 8 garlic cloves, sliced
- 1 tablespoon of spicy bean sauce
- 1 tablespoon of light soy sauce
- 5 tablespoons of vegetable oil
- 6 ginger slices
- ½ teaspoon of sugar
- 5 long hot peppers, sliced

Directions:

1. Sauté the mushrooms, ginger, and garlic with oil in a suitable wok for 5 minutes.
2. Stir in the bean sauce, soy sauce, sugar, and hot peppers.
3. Mix thoroughly and simmer for approximately about 5 minutes on low heat, covered. Serve warm.

Recipe 58: Peking Duck

Serving Size: 6

Preparation Time: 20 minutes

Cooking Time: 1 hour and 45 minutes

Ingredients:

- 1 slice of ginger, fresh
- 1 tablespoon of vinegar, white
- 5-6 pound of duck, whole
- 1 halved scallion
- 8 cups of water, filtered
- 3 tablespoons of honey, pure
- 1 tablespoon of sherry, dry
- 1 & 1/2 tablespoons of corn starch – dissolve in 3 tablespoons of filtered water

Directions:

1. Clean up after the duck. Wipe it clean. Tie a thread around the neck of the duck.
2. For four hours, hang the duck in a breezy, cool location or an unheated room with a fan.
3. Fill a big wok halfway with filtered water. Bring the water to a boil. Mix in the cherry, vinegar, honey, scallions, and ginger. Bring to a boil again. While continually swirling, pour in the dissolved corn starch.
4. Place the duck in a big strainer over a large basin. For approximately about 10-12 minutes, spoon the boiling mixture over the duck.
5. Hang the duck in a breezy, cool location or an unheated room with a fan until completely dry.
6. Place the duck with breast side facing up on greased rack in 350F oven. Set pan with two inches filtered water in bottom of oven. Roast for approximately about 1/2 hour.
7. Turn the duck. Roast for approximately about another 1/2 hour. Turn the duck with breast side facing up once more. Roast for approximately about 10 more minutes.
8. Use sharp knife and cut off crisped skin. Serve skin and meat promptly on warmed dish.

Recipe 59: Pork and Bamboo Shoots

Serving Size: 2

Preparation Time: 15 minutes

Cooking Time: 15 minutes

Ingredients:

- 1 tablespoon of peanut oil
- 2 teaspoons of rice vinegar
- 2 teaspoons of soy sauce
- 3 tablespoons of chicken broth
- 1 can of thinly sliced bamboo shoots
- 2 tablespoons of peanut oil
- 2 cloves of garlic, chopped
- 85 grams of minced pork
- 1 teaspoon of Shaoxing rice wine
- salt to taste
- 3 green onions (thinly sliced)
- 1 teaspoon of sesame oil
- 1 fresh red chilli (seeded and chopped)
- 1/2 teaspoon of crushed red pepper flakes

Directions:

1. Set the wok to medium heat and heat 1 tablespoon of peanut oil. Fry the bamboo shoots in the hot pan for approximately about 3 minutes until fragrant and dry. Remove the bamboo shoots from the stove and set them aside.
2. Turn the heat up to a heat of high and add the remaining peanut oil. Sauté red pepper flakes, garlic, and red chili until fragrant. Add the pork and fry until cooked.
3. Stir in the wine and season with salt. - Put the bamboo shoots back in the wok and heat them until they sizzle. Add the chicken broth, soy sauce, rice vinegar, and salt. Cook, stirring constantly, for 1-2 minutes until the flavors are well blended with the bamboo shoots.
4. Add the spring onions and remove the mixture from the heat. Serve drizzled with sesame oil.

Recipe 60: Pork Fried Rice

Serving Size: 4

Preparation Time: 10 minutes

Cooking Time: 25 minutes

Ingredients:

- 1 tablespoon of water, hot
- 1 teaspoon of honey
- 2 eggs, large and scrambled
- ½ cup of bean sprouts, fresh
- 2 scallions, thinly sliced
- 1 teaspoon of sesame oil
- 1 tablespoon of soy sauce
- 1 teaspoon of soy sauce, dark
- ¼ teaspoon of white pepper
- 5 cups of jasmine rice, cooked
- 1 tablespoon of extra virgin olive oil
- 1 onion, diced
- 1 pound of Chinese BBQ pork, cut into small pieces
- 1 teaspoon of salt
- 1 teaspoon of wine, Shaoxing and optional

Directions:

1. Use a small bowl and add in the water, honey, sesame oil, wine and both of the soy sauces. Season with a dash of white pepper. Stir well to mix.
2. Fluff the pre-cooked jasmine rice using a fork.
3. Place a large wok over medium heat. Add in a spoonful of oil and once the oil is hot enough add in the onions. cook for approximately about 5 minutes or until soft.
4. Add in the roasted pork and cooked rice. Stir well to mix and continue to cook for approximately about 5 minutes.
5. Next, add in the sauce mixture and toss well to coat.
6. Finally, add in the large eggs, bean sprouts and sliced scallions. Stir again to mix and continue to cook for approximately about an additional minute.
7. Remove from heat and serve while piping hot.

Recipe 61: Pork with Veggies

Serving Size: 4

Preparation Time: 15 minutes

Cooking Time: 15 minutes

Ingredients:

- 1-pound pork loin, cut into thin strips
- 1 teaspoon of fresh ginger, minced
- 2 tablespoons of low-sodium soy sauce
- 2 tablespoons of olive oil, divided
- 1 teaspoon of garlic, minced
- 10 ounces broccoli florets
- 1 carrot, peeled and sliced
- 1 tablespoon of fresh lemon juice
- 1 tablespoon of Erythritol
- 1 teaspoon of arrowroot starch
- 1 large red bell pepper, seeded and strips
- 2 scallions, cut into 2-inch pieces

Directions:

1. In a bowl, mix well pork strips, ½ tablespoon of olive oil, garlic, and ginger.
2. For sauce; add the soy sauce, lemon juice, Erythritol, and arrowroot starch in a small bowl and mix well.
3. Heat the remaining olive oil in a large nonstick wok over high heat and sear the pork strips for approximately about 3-4 minutes or until cooked through.
4. With a slotted spoon, transfer the pork into a bowl.
5. In the same wok, add the carrot and cook for approximately about 2-3 minutes.
6. Add the broccoli, bell pepper, and scallion and cook, covered for approximately about 1-2 minutes.
7. Stir the cooked pork and sauce, and cook for approximately about 3-5 minutes or until desired doneness, stirring occasionally.
8. Remove from the heat and serve.

Recipe 62: Potato Chips

Serving Size: 2

Preparation Time: 20 minutes

Cooking Time: 40 minutes

Ingredients:

- 2 tablespoons of distilled white vinegar
- 2 quarts peanut or canola oil
- Kosher salt, as required, to taste
- 1 pound russet potatoes, sliced into 1/8" thick then, rinsed under cold water, cleaned well

Directions:

1. Bring 2 quarts of water and vinegar to a boil in a large saucepan over high heat. Once done, carefully add the slices of potatoes & cook for approximately about 2 to 3 minutes. Spread the slices on a large-sized rimmed baking sheet lined with paper towel to drain, evenly spaced. Let dry for a couple of minutes.
2. Meanwhile, heat the oil in a Dutch oven or big wok over medium heat until it is hot. Add 1/3 of slices of potato & cook for approximately about 10 to 20 minutes, until you hardly see any bubbles, stirring & flipping the slices constantly using a slotted spoon or wire mesh spider, don't burn them. Transfer the cooked chips to a paper towels lined, large-sized bowl and then, sprinkle with salt, gently toss to coat the chips.
3. Transfer the seasoned chips to a large-sized serving bowl & repeat these cooking steps with the leftover slices of potato. Serve immediately and enjoy.

Recipe 63: Potato Curry with Tamarind

Serving Size: 3

Preparation Time: 30 minutes

Cooking Time: 40 minutes

Ingredients:

- 3 dried hot red chillies, stems removed
- 1/2 teaspoon of saltan
- 2 Turkish bay leaves
- 1/4 cup of boiling water
- 3/4 teaspoon of Panch Phoron
- 1 cup of water plus
- 3 tablespoons of vegetable oil
- 1/8 teaspoon of Asafetida powder
- 1 1/2 teaspoons of tamarind concentrate
- 1 tablespoon of cumin seeds
- 1/2 teaspoon of ground turmeric
- 450 g medium-sized jacket potatoes (approx. 5)

Directions:

1. In a dry, small, heavy skillet, toast the chilies and cumin, shaking the skillet occasionally until fragrant and slightly darkened, about 1 minute. Remove from heat and allow to cool, then finely grind in a meat grinder. In a 2 1/2 to 3-quarter saucepan, cover the prepared potatoes with cold, salted water, bring to a boil, then simmer, partially covered, until potatoes are actually tender when pierced with a small sharp knife, about 12 minutes .
2. Drain them. Once the potatoes have cooled sufficiently, use a small sharp knife or vegetable peeler to peel and cut into chunks. Heat the prepared oil in a wok over medium-high heat until hot but not smoking. Add the bay leaves, panchphoron, and asafetida and cook, stirring frequently, until the seeds of the panchphoron are no longer bubbling, about 1 minute. Add potatoes and turmeric and stir-fry until potatoes are light golden brown (3 to 5 minutes).
3. Add 1 cup of water and bring to a boil, then simmer for 5 minutes, stirring occasionally. 5 minutes, while the potatoes are simmering, whisk together the boiling water and tamarind. Season 3 potatoes with salt, 2 teaspoons of cumin chili powder, and tamarind mixture and simmer, stirring occasionally, until gravy thickens slightly thickened (2 to 3 minutes).
4. Seasoning with salt. Discard the bay leaves. Note: Leftover caraway chili powder can be stored in an airtight container at an actual room temperature for up to 3 months.

Recipe 64: Potato Stir Fry

Serving Size: 2

Preparation Time: 10 minutes

Cooking Time: 20 minutes

Ingredients:

- 1 teaspoon of chili flakes
- 1 tablespoon of mustard oil
- Salt to taste
- 1 white onion, chopped
- 2 cups of diced potatoes
- 2 garlic cloves, minced
- Fresh coriander, chopped
- 2 green chilies
- 1 teaspoon of cumin
- ½ teaspoon of black cumin seeds

Directions:

1. In a wok, heat the mustard oil. Add the black cumin seeds and cook for approximately about only 20 seconds.
2. Add the chopped onion and the minced garlic—Cook for 2 minutes.
3. Add the diced potatoes—Cook for 2 minutes. Add the salt, cumin, green chilies, and chili flakes.
4. Cook for 5 minutes and stir. cook for approximately about another 5 minutes and stir.
5. Add the coriander and take off the heat. Serve with the tortilla.

Recipe 65: Red Fish Curry Soup

Serving Size: 4

Preparation Time: 15 minutes

Cooking Time: 25 minutes

Ingredients:

- 2 onions
- 1 bell pepper
- 3 tablespoon of lime juice
- 2 tablespoons of oil
- 200 ml coconut milk
- 2 cloves of garlic
- 200 g snow peas
- 100 g leaf spinach
- 3 tablespoon of chopped coriander
- 300 ml vegetable stock
- 400 g ready-to-cook fish fillet to taste, e.g. pollack
- 6 tablespoon of soy sauce
- 1 teaspoon of red curry paste
- salt

Directions:

1. Cut the fish into pieces about 2 cm in size. Dice the onions and peppers, chop the garlic. Wash the sugar snap peas and remove the threads if necessary. Wash and spin-dry the spinach and roughly chop. Squeeze the limes.
2. Heat the oil in a non-stick pan or a wok, sear the pieces of fish in it, remove from the pan and set aside.
3. Put the onions, peppers and garlic in the pan, fry briefly. Top up with coconut milk, soy sauce and vegetable stock, bring to the boil. Add the spinach, sugar snap peas and fish. Salt well and season with curry paste. Let simmer for 5 minutes. Add lime juice and sprinkle with coriander greens.

Recipe 66: Salmon and Noodle Stir Fry

Serving Size: 4

Preparation Time: 10 minutes

Cooking Time: 15 minutes

Ingredients:

- 3 tablespoons of vegetable oil
- 12 ounces salmon, cubed
- 1 clove garlic, crushed
- 1/4 cup of honey
- 1/3 cup of soy sauce
- 1/2 red pepper, thinly sliced
- 1 zucchini, thinly sliced
- 17 ounces wholegrain Hokkien noodles
- 2 carrots, thinly sliced
- 3 spring onions, thinly sliced
- 1 bunch bok choi, chopped
- 2 tablespoons of sesame seeds

Directions:

1. Start by placing the Hokkien noodles in a pan, cover with boiling water, cover with a lid, then leave for 5 minutes. Do not put it on the heat. After 5 minutes, they should be soft, so drain off the water and set to one side.
2. In a small bowl, make the sauce by mixing the garlic, soy sauce, and honey.
3. Put a wok on high heat, add in the oil, then toss in the salmon cubes and fry for a couple of minutes on each side until cooked through. Transfer to a plate.
4. Next, throw in the pepper, bok choi, zucchini, and carrots, fry for 2 to 3 minutes, keep moving the veggies around to prevent them from burning.
5. Add in the noodles and the sauce and continue to fry for 5 minutes.
6. Put the salmon back into the wok with the rest of the ingredients and give everything a good shake round to make sure the salmon is coated in the sauce.
7. To serve, sprinkle over the spring onions and sesame seeds.

Recipe 67: Satay Veggie Noodles

Serving Size: 4

Preparation Time: 10 minutes

Cooking Time: 15 minutes

Ingredients:

- 1 tablespoon of brown sugar
- 2 tablespoons of soy sauce
- 1 tablespoon of honey
- 1 tablespoon of canola oil
- 2 cloves of garlic (peeled, sliced thinly)
- ½ teaspoon of salt
- 8 ounces of dried rice noodles
- 4 tablespoons of crunchy peanut butter
- 2 tablespoons of hot water
- 1 teaspoon of Chinese 5-spice
- 1 leek (white only, sliced thinly)
- 1 chili pepper (seeded, minced)
- 4 handfuls of shredded cabbage

Directions:

1. Soak the noodles in warm water for several minutes until al dente. Drain.
2. In a bowl, stir together the peanut butter, how water, sugar, soy sauce, honey, salt, and 5-spice.
3. Warm the oil in a wok over moderate heat. Add the garlic, leek, and chili and sauté for a couple of minutes.
4. Next, add the cabbage and sauté for 60 seconds.
5. Raise the heat to a fairly high setting and add the sauce.
6. When the sauce begins to bubble, add the noodle and toss to coat with the sauce. cook for approximately about a couple of minutes more, or until well heated, and serve immediately.

Recipe 68: Savory Steamed Egg Custard

Serving Size: 4

Preparation Time: 10 minutes

Cooking Time: 10 minutes

Ingredients:

- ½ teaspoon of kosher salt
- 4 large eggs, at room temperature
- 2 teaspoons of Shaoxing rice wine
- 2 scallions, green part only, thinly sliced
- 1¾ cups of low-sodium chicken broth or filtered water
- 4 teaspoons of sesame oil

Directions:

1. In a large bowl, whisk the eggs. Add the broth and rice wine and whisk to combine. Strain the prepared egg mixture through a fine-mesh sieve set over a liquid measuring cup of to remove air bubbles. Pour the egg mixture into 4 (6-ounce) ramekins. With a paring knife, pop any bubbles on the surface of the egg mixture. Cover the ramekins with aluminum foil.
2. Rinse a bamboo steamer basket and its lid under cold water and place it in the wok. Pour in 2 inches of water, or until it comes above the bottom rim of the steamer by ¼ to ½ inch, but not so much that it touches the bottom of the basket. Place the ramekins in the steamer basket. Cover with the lid.
3. Bring the water to a very hot boil, then reduce the heat to an actual low simmer. Steam over low heat for approximately about 10 minutes or until the eggs are just set.
4. Carefully remove the ramekins from the steamer and garnish each custard with some scallions and a few drops of sesame oil. Serve immediately.

Recipe 69: Shanghai Spring Rolls

Serving Size: 12

Preparation Time: 20 minutes

Cooking Time: 20 minutes

Ingredients:

- 2 tablespoons of Shaoxing wine
- 8 dried shiitake mushrooms, soaked
- ½ teaspoon of soy sauce
- 1 ½ tablespoon of cornstarch
- 1 tablespoon of water
- ⅔ cup of shredded lean pork
- 1 small Napa cabbage, shredded
- 4 tablespoons of oil
- Salt, to taste
- 2 teaspoons of sesame oil
- 24 roll wrappers
- White pepper, to taste
- Oil, for frying

Directions:

1. Mix the pork, cabbage, mushrooms, and the rest of the ingredients in a bowl, except for the roll wrappers. In a decent wok, sauté the filling for around 10 minutes.
2. Allow the filling to cool somewhat before spreading the egg roll wrappers out on the work area. In the middle of each wrapper, divide the pork filling.
3. Wet the wrapper's edges, fold the two sides in half, then roll the wrappers into an egg roll.
4. Preheat the oil to a heat of 325 degrees F in a deep wok, then deep fried the egg rolls until golden brown.
5. Transfer the golden egg rolls to a paper towel-lined dish. Warm the dish before serving.

Recipe 70: Shiitake Mushrooms with Spring Onions

Serving Size: 4

Preparation Time: 20 minutes

Cooking Time: 20 minutes

Ingredients:

- 1/2 teaspoon of salt
- 1/4 teaspoon of white pepper
- 1 tablespoon of peanut oil
- 200 g sliced bacon, cut crosswise into pieces
- 4 large garlic cloves, thinly sliced
- 2 cups of chicken broth
- 12 spring onions (white and light green parts only), smashed with a heavy knife and roughly chopped
- 450g fresh shiitake mushrooms, stems removed

Directions:

1. Heat a prepared wok or 12-inch skillet over high heat until a bead of water that dripped onto the stovetop immediately evaporates. Add the oil, toss in the wok and heat until it begins to smoke. Add the bacon and stir-fry until brown and crispy, about 3 minutes.
2. Place on paper towels with a slotted spoon, drain and save for another use. Add the spring onions and garlic to the bacon and stir-fry, stirring, until fragrant, 1 minute.
3. Pour the broth into the wok (it will bubble vigorously), add salt and white pepper and bring to a boil.
4. Add the mushrooms, then reduce the heat and simmer, covered, until tender, about 5 minutes, turning occasionally.
5. Using a slotted spoon, place the mushrooms in a bowl and when cool, slice. If desired, you can drizzle the mushrooms with liquid.

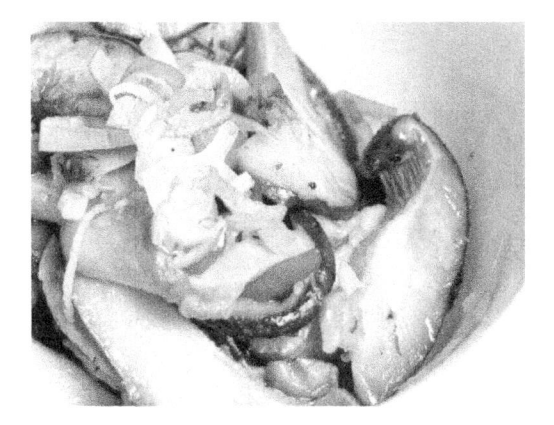

Recipe 71: Shrimp and Cabbage Stir-Fry

Serving Size: 4

Preparation Time: 15 minutes

Cooking Time: 15 minutes

Ingredients:

- 2 tablespoons vegetable oil
- 1 large egg white
- 1 tablespoon plus 1 teaspoon soy sauce
- 2 teaspoons hoisin sauce
- 1 1/4 pounds medium shrimp, peeled and deveined
- 1 1/2 teaspoons of sherry vinegar or rice wine vinegar
- 1/2 cup low-sodium chicken broth or water
- 4 scallions, cut into 1/2-inch pieces, white and green parts separated
- 1 tablespoon finely grated peeled ginger
- 1 tablespoon of plus 2 teaspoons cornstarch
- 1 clove garlic, finely grated
- 1 pound Napa cabbage (1/2 head), cut into 1-inch pieces
- Cooked white rice, for serving (optional)

Directions:

1. Whisk the egg white, 1 tablespoon of cornstarch and 1 teaspoon soy sauce in a large bowl until frothy. Add the shrimp and toss to coat. Refrigerate 10 minutes. Meanwhile, whisk the hoisin sauce, vinegar and the remaining 1 tablespoon of soy sauce and 2 teaspoons cornstarch in a small bowl, then whisk in the chicken broth. Set aside.
2. Drain the shrimp. Heat the vegetable oil in a wok or large skillet over medium-high heat, then stir-fry the scallion whites, ginger and garlic, about 30 seconds. Add the shrimp and stir-fry until almost cooked through, about 3 minutes. Add the cabbage and stir-fry until wilted and the shrimp are just cooked through, about 2 more minutes.
3. Stir the hoisin sauce mixture, then add to the wok and simmer, stirring occasionally, 2 minutes. Stir in the scallion greens. Serve with rice, if desired.

Recipe 72: Shrimp and Squid Stir-Fry with Bok Choy

Serving Size: 4

Preparation Time: 10 minutes

Cooking Time: 5 minutes

Ingredients:

- 8 ounces squid tentacles and/or rings
- 2 tablespoons of cornstarch, divided
- 2 tablespoons of cooking oil
- 1 tablespoon of chopped fresh ginger
- 4 tablespoons of Shaoxing cooking wine, divided
- 4 tablespoons of light soy sauce, divided
- 2 tablespoons of toasted sesame oil, divided
- 2 garlic cloves, crushed and chopped
- 8 ounces large shrimp, shelled, deveined, and cut in half lengthwise
- 1 (15-ounce) can straw mushrooms, drained and rinsed
- 2 cups of bok choy cut into ½-inch pieces
- 4 scallions, both white and green parts, cut into ¼-inch pieces
- Rice or noodles, for serving

Directions:

1. In two medium bowls, velvet the shrimp and squid separately by combining half the wine, soy sauce, sesame oil, and cornstarch in each bowl.
2. In the wok, heat the cooking oil over medium-high heat until it shimmers.
3. Add the ginger, garlic, and shrimp, reserving any liquid, and stir-fry for 2 minutes, until fragrant.
4. Add the mushrooms and stir-fry for 1 minute, until the shrimp is opaque.
5. Add the prepared bok choy and stir-fry for 1 minute, until bright green.
6. Add the squid and stir-fry for 1 minute, reserving any liquid, until the squid curls.
7. Add the remaining liquids and scallions and stir-fry for 1 minute to form a light glaze. Serve over rice or noodles.

Recipe 73: Shrimp Lo Mein with Broccoli

Serving Size: 2

Preparation Time: 10 minutes

Cooking Time: 25 minutes

Ingredients:

- 2 tablespoons of soy sauce
- 2 tablespoons of brown sugar
- 2 teaspoons of fish sauce
- 1 (8-ounce) package spaghetti
- 3 medium Cremini mushrooms, sliced
- 2 tablespoons of oyster sauce
- ½ teaspoon of garlic powder
- 2 teaspoons of vegetable oil
- 2 cloves garlic, minced
- ½ teaspoon of ground ginger
- 1 pound of Uncooked medium shrimp, peeled & deveined
- 1 cup of broccoli, chopped
- ¼ yellow onion, thinly sliced
- 2 large eggs

Directions:

1. Bring a large-sized pot of salted water to a boil and cook the prepared spaghetti according to package directions, and then drain.
2. Mix your oyster sauce, soy sauce, fish sauce, brown sugar, garlic powder and ground ginger in a bowl until the sugar dissolves.
3. Heat the oil in large wok over medium heat setting. Stir in your shrimp until they change color or for approximately about 2 minutes.
4. Add the onion, broccoli and mushrooms, then cook until they begin to soften or for approximately about 5 minutes. Stir the garlic through the veggie mixture. Push veggies to one side of pan.
5. Cook your eggs in the open space in pan, scramble lightly or until no longer moist for approximately about 5-minutes.
6. Stir your cooked egg with veggies and shrimp. Add the prepared cooked noodles and sauce and stir until well combined or for approximately about 2 minutes. Serve and enjoy!

Recipe 74: Shrimp with Lobster Sauce

Serving Size: 4

Preparation Time: 15 minutes

Cooking Time: 30 minutes

Ingredients:

- 1 1/2 teaspoons of cornstarch
- 2 teaspoons of cooking sherry
- 2 cloves garlic, minced
- 1/4 pound of ground pork
- 4 tablespoons of vegetable oil
- 2 tablespoons of soy sauce
- 1/4 teaspoon of sugar
- 1/2 teaspoon of salt
- 1 cup of water
- 1 pound of medium shrimp - peeled and deveined
- 1 1/2 tablespoons of cornstarch
- 1/4 cup of cold water
- 1 egg, beaten

Directions:

1. Mix a teaspoon of and a half of cornstarch in the sherry in a medium bowl. Stir until well dissolved. Toss the shrimp in the basin to coat.
2. In a large pot or wok set over medium-high heat, heat up oil. Cook shrimps for 3 to 5 minutes until pink. Using a slotted utensil, remove shrimp and transfer to a plate, leaving as much oil in the pot as possible. Cook garlic in the reserved oil for a few seconds; mix in ground pork. Stir constantly until the pork is no longer pink. Combine sugar, salt, a cup of water, and soy sauce. Add the mixture to the pot. Allow the combined mixture to come to a boil, then cover and reduce the heat to medium. Let it simmer for approximately about 2 minutes. In a separate medium-sized bowl, mix a quarter cup of cold water and 1 1/2 tablespoons of cornstarch. Pour the mixture into the pan; add the shrimps. Let it simmer; pour beaten egg slowly while stirring quickly. Serve hot over rice.

Recipe 75: Sirloin Stir-Fry with Ramen Noodles

Serving Size: 4

Preparation Time: 10 minutes

Cooking Time: 20 minutes

Ingredients:

- 2 tablespoons of cornstarch
- 2 cups of beef broth, divided
- ½ cup of unsalted peanuts
- 2 cups of fresh broccoli florets
- 2 (14-ounce) cans whole baby corn, rinsed & drained
- 2 tablespoons of low-sodium soy sauce
- 4 green onions, sliced into 1-inch pieces
- 2 packages (3-0unce each) beef Ramen noodles
- 1 cup of shredded carrots
- 1 cup of sweet red pepper, diced
- 2 tablespoons of canola oil
- 1 pound of beef top sirloin steak, cut into very thin strips

Directions:

1. Place packets of seasoning for noodles aside. Cook your noodles according to package directions. In a small bowl, combine your cornstarch and ¼ cup of broth until smooth, then set aside.
2. Stir fry your beef in large wok in oil until no longer pink or for approximately about 5 minutes. Add your soy sauce to wok and cook until liquid has evaporated. Remove the beef from heat and keep warm.
3. Add your corn, carrots, red pepper, onions and broccoli into the pan along with remaining broth. Add in the seasoning packets contents and stir-fry until veggies are crisp for approximately about 7 minutes.
4. Add your cornstarch mixture to the wok and bring to a boil, cook until thickened for approximately about 2-minutes. Drain Ramen noodles, then add the beef and noodles to wok and heat through. Serve and enjoy!

Recipe 76: Smoked-Tea Tilapia

Serving Size: 4

Preparation Time: 10 minutes

Cooking Time: 15 minutes

Ingredients:

- 1 tablespoon of toasted sesame oil
- ¼ cup of uncooked long-grain white rice
- 1 pound fresh tilapia fillets (3 or 4 fillets)
- 2 tablespoons of Shaoxing cooking wine
- 2 tablespoons of brown sugar
- 2 tablespoons of light soy sauce
- ¼ cup of loose black oolong tea
- Rice, for serving
- Vegetables, for serving

Directions:

1. In a zip-top bag, combine the tilapia, wine, soy sauce, and sesame oil and massage to cover it on all sides.
2. Combine the rice, tea leaves, and brown sugar on a square piece of aluminum foil and roll the edges up to form the foil into a shallow, ½-inch-deep saucer. The top should be open. Place the foil saucer in the bottom of the wok.
3. Place a rack in the wok and put the fish on the rack above the mixture. Cover with a domed lid.
4. If you're cooking indoors, open any windows near the stove and turn your exhaust fan on high. If you don't have a way to exhaust air outside, do the next steps outdoors.
5. Turn the heat on high. As the mixture heats, it will begin to smoke. First the smoke will be white, then light yellow, then darker yellow. When it turns dark yellow (about 5 minutes), turn the heat to low.
6. Allow the fish to smoke on low for 5 minutes, then turn the actual heat off and wait 5 minutes before checking the fish. It will be dark golden brown and flaky.
7. Serve over rice with a side of vegetables.

Recipe 77: Soup Dumplings

Serving Size: 2
Preparation Time: 55 minutes
Cooking Time: 10 minutes

Ingredients:

- 1 cup of hot tap water
- 1 teaspoon of chopped fresh ginger
- 1 garlic clove, crushed and chopped
- 4 ounces ground pork
- 2 scallions, minced
- 1 teaspoon of soy sauce
- 1 teaspoon of sugar
- 1 teaspoon of toasted sesame oil
- 1 teaspoon of chicken, beef, or pork bouillon
- 1 (¼-ounce) package unflavored gelatin
- 20 (4-inch) round dumpling wrappers (If you use smaller wrappers, they will be harder to fold)
- 4 to 6 lettuce leaves

Directions:

1. In a medium bowl, combine the hot tap water, bouillon, and gelatin, and mix until the gelatin dissolves. Put in the refrigerator or freezer until gelatinized.
2. In a large bowl, combine the pork, scallions, ginger, garlic, soy sauce, sugar, and sesame oil and mix well.
3. Transfer the gelatinized broth to the meat mixture and combine.
4. Place about 1 tablespoon of filling in the center of the wrapper, being careful not to get any filling on the outer ¼-inch edge of the wrapper.
5. Create a dumpling by holding the wrapper in your nondominant hand and making pleats with your dominant hand, rotating the wrapper as you go, and bringing the dough together to look like a "moneybag." When you get to the end, seal the wrapper by twisting the top.
6. Line the steamer basket with the lettuce leaves and place the dumplings on the lettuce. Repeat with the remaining filling and wrappers.
7. Fill the wok with about 2 inches of water and place the steamer basket in the wok. The water level should be above the bottom rim of the steamer by ¼ to ½ inch, but not so high that it touches the bottom of the basket. Cover the basket with the steamer basket lid and bring the water to a very hot boil over medium-high heat.
8. Reduce the heat to medium and steam for 10 minutes, or until cooked through.
9. Poke with a chopstick and slurp immediately. Be careful! The soup inside the dumplings will be actually very hot.

Recipe 78: Spicy Honey Sesame Chicken and Broccoli Stir-Fry

Serving Size: 4

Preparation Time: 10 minutes

Cooking Time: 5 minutes

Ingredients:

- 1 teaspoon of spicy sesame oil
- 2 tablespoons of Shaoxing cooking wine
- 2 tablespoons of cooking oil
- 1 tablespoon of chopped, fresh ginger
- 2 tablespoons of light soy sauce
- 1 tablespoon of cornstarch
- 3 garlic cloves, crushed and chopped
- 2 cups of broccoli florets
- 1 pound of boneless, skinless chicken thighs, ¼-inch pieces across the grain
- ¼ cup of honey
- 4 scallions, both white and green parts, cut into ¼-inch pieces, for garnishing
- 1 tablespoon of toasted sesame seeds, for garnishing
- Rice or noodles, for serving

Directions:

1. In a prepared medium bowl, combine the chicken thighs, sesame oil, wine, soy sauce, and cornstarch.
2. In the wok, heat the cooking oil over medium-high heat until it shimmers. Add the ginger, garlic, and chicken thighs, reserving the liquid. Stir-fry for 2 minutes, until fragrant and browned.
3. Add the broccoli and stir-fry for approximately about 1 minute, until bright green.
4. Add the honey and the remaining liquid from the chicken and stir-fry for 1 minute, until the chicken is cooked through and broccoli is tender-crisp.
5. Garnish with the scallions and sesame seeds. Serve over rice or noodles.

Recipe 79: Spicy Poached Beef

Serving Size: 4

Preparation Time: 15 minutes

Cooking Time: 5 minutes

Ingredients:

- 1 teaspoon of spicy sesame oil
- 1 tablespoon of oyster sauce
- 1 tablespoon of Chinese five-spice powder
- 3 garlic cloves, crushed and chopped
- 1 tablespoon of soy sauce
- 1 tablespoon of Shaoxing cooking wine
- ¼ cup of plus 1 tablespoon of cornstarch, divided
- 2 tablespoons of cooking oil
- 1 tablespoon of chopped fresh ginger
- 1 pound thin-sliced sirloin steak, cut across the grain
- 2 cups of gai lan (Chinese broccoli), cut into 2-inch pieces
- 2 cups of broth (meat, seafood, or vegetable)
- 1 (15-ounce) can straw mushrooms, drained and rinsed
- 4 scallions, both white and green parts, cut into ¼-inch pieces, for garnishing

Directions:

1. In a bowl, combine the steak, sesame oil, five-spice powder, soy sauce, wine, oyster sauce, and ¼ cup of cornstarch, and mix well.
2. In the wok, heat the cooking oil over high heat until it shimmers.
3. Add the ginger, garlic, and gai lan, and stir-fry for 1 minute, until fragrant.
4. Add the broth and the mushrooms, and bring to a simmer.
5. Stir the steak again to be sure it is well coated, then add it to the simmering broth.
6. Let the steak simmer for 2 minutes, then stir in the remaining 1 tablespoon of cornstarch to thicken slightly.
7. Garnish with the scallions and serve over rice or noodles.

Recipe 80: Spicy Tempeh Fries

Serving Size: 2

Preparation Time: 10 minutes

Cooking Time: 10 minutes

Ingredients:

- 1 cup of tempeh
- 2 tablespoons of sweet soy sauce
- 2 red chilies, chopped
- A pinch of pepper
- A pinch of salt
- A pinch of red chili powder

Directions:

1. Peel and thinly slice the tempeh.
2. Season the tempeh with salt, pepper, and red chili powder, then toss to combine.
3. Melt the butter in a wok.
4. Toss in the tempeh for 2 minutes.
5. Toss in the soy sauce and red chile for 5 minutes.
6. Serve immediately.

Recipe 81: Spicy Vegetable Lo Mein

Serving Size: 4

Preparation Time: 20 minutes

Cooking Time: 35 minutes

Ingredients:

- 8 ounces of lo mein noodles
- 1 teaspoon of sesame oil
- 2 tablespoons of peanut oil, divided
- 1 tablespoon of minced fresh ginger
- 2 tablespoons of reduced-sodium soy sauce
- 1 tablespoon of Shao Hsing rice wine (see Tips) or dry sherry
- 1 tablespoon of sriracha or other Asian hot sauce
- 12 ounces of Chinese broccoli (see Tips) or broccolini
- 1 tablespoon of minced garlic
- 6 ounces of fresh shiitake mushrooms, thinly sliced
- Pinch of salt

Directions:

1. Boil 2-quarts of water in a large pot. Stir in noodles and cook according to package directions. Drain and then rinse the cooked noodles under cold running water, shaking them well to remove any excess water. Put the noodles on a cutting board and cut coarsely into thirds. Put noodles back in the large pot and mix with sesame oil; set aside.
2. Cut off 1/4-inch of the broccoli, or broccoli, stalks. If the stalks are thicker than 1/2 inch, cut them in half lengthwise. Separate stalks and leaves and cut them into 2-inch long pieces. In a small bowl, mix soy sauce, hot sauce, and rice wine or sherry.
3. Place a 14-inch flat-bottomed wok or large skillet (don't use nonstick) over high heat and heat until a water drop vaporizes immediately after 1-2 seconds of contact. Pour in 1 tablespoon of peanut oil and add the garlic and ginger. Cook and stir for approximately about 10 seconds until fragrant. Stir in broccoli (or broccoli) stalks and mushrooms and cook for approximately about 30 seconds until oil is completely absorbed. Pour the remaining 1 tablespoon of oil and add the broccoli leaves and noodles. Mix and cook until just combined, 15 seconds. Stir in soy sauce mixture. Season with salt and simmer for another 1-2 minutes, or until the noodles are well warm.

Recipe 82: Spinach and Glass Noodle Salad

Serving Size: 2

Preparation Time: 10 minutes

Cooking Time: 20 minutes

Ingredients:

- 3 garlic cloves, minced
- 3 tablespoons of canola oil
- 1 tablespoon of black vinegar
- 1 teaspoon of Chinese light soy sauce
- ½ teaspoon of sea salt
- ½ teaspoon of granulated sugar
- 1 (1½ oz / 40g) bunch glass noodles, soaked in cool water for 15 minutes
- 12 cups of (14oz / 400g) lightly packed spinach, cut into 2-inch-long pieces
- 1 tablespoon of red Sichuan peppercorns
- 3 dried red facing heaven chili peppers, cut into ¼-inch segments

Directions:

1. Set up two bowls of cold water. Over high heat, bring a large-sized saucepan of water to a boil. Add the noodles and blanch for 4 minutes, then scoop them out of the water (without draining the pot) and transfer them to one of the bowls of cold water to cool.
2. In the same pot, blanch the spinach for 1½ minutes. Drain the long pieces of spinach and set it aside to chill in a second basin of cold water.
3. Drain the glass noodles, then use a pair of scissors to cut them into 6-inch-long pieces. Drain the spinach in a colander, then squeeze out as much water as possible.
4. In a medium bowl, combine the noodles, vinegar, soy sauce, salt, and sugar. Put the spinach on top of the noodles and pile the garlic on top.
5. Heat the oil, Sichuan peppercorns, and chilies in a wok for 2 minutes over medium heat, or just until the spices are actually toasted and the oil starts to smoke. Discard the chilies and peppercorns and immediately pour the hot oil over the garlic in the bowl.
6. Mix all the ingredients together. Serve as an appetizer or side dish.

Recipe 83: Steamed Pork Dumplings

Serving Size: 30

Preparation Time: 20 minutes

Cooking Time: 1 hour

Ingredients:

- 1 cm piece ginger, peeled, finely chopped
- 3/4 teaspoon of sesame oil
- 1/4 teaspoon of white pepper
- 2 garlic cloves, crushed
- 4 green onions, chopped
- 2 teaspoons of Chinese rice wine
- 3 teaspoons of white sugar
- 1/4 cup of bamboo shoots, chopped
- 1 tablespoon of coriander leaves, chopped
- 1 1/2 tablespoons of white wine vinegar
- 1/4 cup of soy sauce
- 30 fresh wonton wrappers
- 300 grams of pork mince

Directions:

1. Mix onion, garlic, pork, rice wine, bamboo shoot, white pepper, oil, and salt in a mixing bowl. Put a teaspoon of mixture onto each wonton, dampen edges with water, then form a triangle shape and seal.
2. Fill the wok with water until a quarter full and simmer over high heat. Move steamer with baking paper on base over the wok, then steam dumplings for 15 to 20 minutes.
3. In a small bowl, mix vinegar, soy sauce, sugar, coriander, and ginger until evenly combined. Serve.

Recipe 84: Steamed Tempeh with Chinese Broccoli in Hoisin Sauce

Serving Size: 4

Preparation Time: 10 minutes

Cooking Time: 10 minutes

Ingredients:

- 1 cup of water
- ¼ cup of hoisin sauce
- 1 tablespoon of toasted sesame oil
- 1 pound tempeh, cut into ½-inch cubes
- 2 cups of gai lan (Chinese broccoli) cut into 2-inch pieces
- Rice or noodles, for serving

Directions:

1. In the wok, bring the water to a boil over high heat. Place a rack in the wok.
2. In a pie pan or shallow dish, toss the tempeh and hoisin sauce together. Place the dish on the rack.
3. Cover and steam for 8 minutes.
4. Add the gai lan to the pan and mix with the tempeh; cover and steam for another 2 minutes, until tender-crisp.
5. Drizzle in the sesame oil, toss, and serve over rice or noodles.

Recipe 85: Sticky Rice Pork Balls

Serving Size: 2

Preparation Time: 30 minutes

Cooking Time: 2 hour and 15 minutes

Ingredients:

- 1/2 cups of sticky rice
- 1 piece fresh ginger root, minced
- 2 teaspoons of soy sauce
- salt to taste
- 1 tablespoon of pork stock, or as needed
- 1/4 cup of water, or as needed
- 1 egg
- 4 ounces of ground pork
- 2 tablespoons of cornstarch
- 1 teaspoon of dried goji berries (wolfberries), or to taste

Directions:

1. Wash the sticky rice then put it in a bowl and add water to cover it. Allow for at least 3 hours of soak time before draining.
2. Put the egg in a big bowl then beat it. Pour in the soy sauce, ginger root, and salt and mix. Mix in cornstarch, pork stock, and pork then stir in just one direction for 5-6 minutes until blended. Form bite-size balls by rolling the pork mixture in portions.
3. Fill the wok with about 1 inch of water then simmer.
4. Coat the pork balls by rolling them in the sticky rice until they are completely coated. In a steamer basket, put 6 balls in.
5. Put the steamer in the wok and let the balls steam for 30 minutes until the rice becomes tender and the pork is thoroughly cooked. Take the balls out of the steamer and add goji berries for garnishing.

Recipe 86: Stir-Fried Bok Choy and Mushrooms

Serving Size: 3

Preparation Time: 10 minutes

Cooking Time: 10 minutes

Ingredients:

- 3 tablespoons of vegetable oil
- Kosher salt
- 2 garlic cloves, minced
- 2 teaspoons of light soy sauce
- 2 teaspoons of sesame oil
- ½ pound fresh shiitake mushrooms, stems removed and caps cut into quarters
- 1 ½ pounds baby bok choy, sliced crosswise into 1-inch pieces
- 1 peeled fresh ginger slice, about the size of a quarter
- 2 tablespoons of Shaoxing rice wine

Directions:

1. Heat a wok over medium-high heat until a drop of water sizzles and evaporates on contact. Pour in the vegetable oil and swirl to coat the base of the wok. Season the oil by adding the ginger slice and a pinch of salt. Allow the ginger to sizzle in the oil for approximately about 30 seconds, swirling gently.
2. Add the mushrooms and stir-fry for 3 to 4 minutes, until they just begin to brown. Add the garlic and stir-fry until fragrant, approximately about 30 seconds more.
3. Add the bok choy and toss with the mushrooms. The wok may appear crowded, but the bok choy will wilt down quickly. Add the rice wine, light soy, and sesame oil. cook for approximately about 3 to 4 minutes, tossing the vegetables constantly until they are tender.
4. Transfer the vegetables to a serving platter, discard the ginger, and serve hot.

Recipe 87: Stir-Fried Pork with Sweet Bean Paste

Serving Size: 2

Preparation Time: 15 minutes

Cooking Time: 26 minutes

Ingredients:

- 2 tablespoons of water
- 2 teaspoons of salt, divided
- 3 tablespoons of water
- 1 teaspoon of white sugar
- 1 teaspoon of soy sauce
- 1 teaspoon of cornstarch
- 9 ounces of pork, cut into thin strips
- 3 1/2 tablespoons of vegetable oil
- 2 tablespoons of sweet bean paste
- 1/8 teaspoon of monosodium glutamate (MSG)
- 2 spring onions (white parts only), cut into matchstick-size pieces

Directions:

1. Combine cornstarch and 2 tablespoons of water in a bowl and stir them together.
2. In a shallow dish or bowl, place the pork in then add in 1 teaspoon of salt and the cornstarch mixture. Coat the pork by stirring then allow to sit for several minutes.
3. In a bowl, combine 3 tablespoons of water, soy sauce, sugar, 1 teaspoon of salt, and MSG and mix them together until the sauce is smooth.
4. Pour oil in a big cooking pan or wok and heat it on medium-high heat. Add the pork and sauté it in the oil for 5 minutes until it's thoroughly cooked. Add the sweet bean paste after pushing the pork to the side of the wok or pan. Cook the bean paste while stirring for a minute until it's fragrant. Add the sauce in and stir for approximately about 2-3 minutes until it has thickened.
5. Move the pork mixture to a platter or dish and add spring onions as toppings.

Recipe 88: Sui Mai Dumplings

Serving Size: 40

Preparation Time: 40 minutes

Cooking Time: 15 minutes

Ingredients:

- 8 ounces ground pork
- 1 teaspoon of soy sauce
- 4 ounces shrimp, peeled and deveined
- 1 tablespoon of sugar
- 1 tablespoon of Shaoxing cooking wine
- 3 dried shiitake mushrooms, soaked and minced; tough stems removed if using whole mushrooms
- 1 (12-ounce) package round wonton wrappers

Directions:

1. In a food processor, combine and pulse together the mushrooms, pork, sugar, wine, and soy sauce.
2. Add the shrimp and coarsely chop until evenly mixed in.
3. To assemble dumplings, make an "O" with your thumb and forefinger. Place a wrapper over the O and gently push a teaspoon of the filling along with the wrapper down into the O.
4. Use a butter knife to gently press and spread more filling so it is level to the top edge of the wrapper.
5. Press the bottom onto the work surface to flatten it, and use your fingers to make the dumpling cylindrical.
6. Line a steamer with parchment paper and place the dumplings on the tray. Repeat with remaining filling and wrappers.
7. Fill the wok with about 2 inches of water and place the steamer in the wok. The water level should be above the bottom rim of the steamer by ¼ to ½ inch, but not so high that it touches the bottom of the basket. Cover the steamer with the lid and bring the water to a very hot boil over medium-high heat.
8. Reduce the heat to medium and steam for 10 minutes, or until cooked through. Serve immediately.

Recipe 89: Tea-Smoked Tofu with Sweet Peppers and Red Onions

Serving Size: 4

Preparation Time: 10 minutes

Cooking Time: 10 minutes

Ingredients:

- 2 tablespoons of light soy sauce
- 2 tablespoons of brown sugar
- 1 medium red bell pepper, 1-inch pieces
- ¼ cup of uncooked long-grain white rice
- ¼ cup of lapsang souchong tea leaves
- 1 medium red onion, 1-inch pieces
- 1 pound firm or extra-firm tofu, drained, patted dry, and cut into 1-inch pieces
- ¼ cup of hoisin sauce
- Rice or noodles, for serving

Directions:

1. In a medium bowl, combine and toss the tofu with soy sauce to coat it.
2. Combine the rice, tea leaves, and brown sugar on a square piece of aluminum foil and roll the edges up to form the foil into a shallow, ½-inch-deep saucer. The top should be open. Place the foil saucer in the bottom of the wok.
3. In a prepared pie pan or shallow dish, combine the tofu, bell pepper, and onion. Place a rack in the wok and the pan on the rack. Cover with a domed lid.
4. If you're cooking indoors, open any windows near the stove and turn your exhaust fan on high. If you don't have a way to exhaust air outside, do the next steps outdoors.
5. Turn the heat on high. As the mixture heats, it will begin to smoke. First the smoke will be white, then light yellow, then darker yellow (about 5 minutes).
6. When the smoke turns dark yellow, wait for 4 minutes, then turn the heat on low for 6 minutes.
7. Turn off the heat. Drizzle the hoisin sauce over the ingredients and toss lightly. Serve over rice or noodles.

Recipe 90: Thai Shrimp Stir-Fry

Serving Size: 4

Preparation Time: 15 minutes

Cooking Time: 10 minutes

Ingredients:

- 1 teaspoon of canola oil
- 1 cup of fresh snow peas
- 1 teaspoon of fresh gingeroot, minced
- 1 tablespoon of rice vinegar
- 1 pound of Uncooked medium shrimp, peeled & deveined
- ½ teaspoon of crushed red pepper flakes
- ½ cup of green onions, thinly sliced
- 4 ½ teaspoons of low-sodium soy sauce
- 2 medium sweet red peppers, sliced into thin slices
- 2 tablespoons of low-fat peanut butter
- 1 garlic clove, minced
- 4 cups of hot cooked fettuccine
- 1 ½ cups of low-sodium vegetable broth

Directions:

1. In a large wok, stir-fry your red peppers in hot canola over medium-high heat for approximately about 1 minute. Add in your snow peas, garlic, green onions, then stir-fry for 3 minutes or until veggies are crisp and tender, remove from heat and keep warm.
2. Add broth, peanut butter, vinegar, soy sauce, sesame oil, pepper flakes, and ginger. Cook and stir peanut butter until mixture comes to a boil. Stir in the shrimp and continue to cook for approximately about another 3 minutes or until shrimp turns pink. Return red pepper mixture to wok, heat, then serve over bed of fettuccine noodles and enjoy!

Recipe 91: Tiger Skin Long Hot Peppers

Serving Size: 4

Preparation Time: 15 minutes

Cooking Time: 20 minutes

Ingredients:

- 1 tablespoon of black vinegar
- 1 teaspoon of dark soy sauce
- 6 garlic cloves, roughly chopped
- 1 teaspoon of granulated sugar
- ½ teaspoon of sea salt
- 1 tablespoon of water
- 1 pound (454g) green long hot peppers
- 2 tablespoons of canola oil
- 2 tablespoons of fermented black beans

Directions:

1. In a small-sized bowl, mix the black vinegar, water, soy sauce, sugar, and salt. Set the sauce aside.
2. Remove the stems from the peppers, cut a long slit down the length of each pepper, and use the slit to remove the seeds. Cut the peppers in half crosswise.
3. Heat a wok over medium-high heat. Add the peppers and press on them with a ladle to char their skins, turning the peppers to char both sides, for approximately about 10 minutes, or until all the peppers are blackened, blistered, and limp. Transfer the peppers to a plate.
4. Reduce the heat to a heat of medium-low and add the oil, garlic, and black beans to the wok. Stir until fragrant. Return the peppers to the wok and increase the heat to high. Add the sauce and stir the peppers for approximately about 30 seconds so they take on the flavor. Serve hot.

Recipe 92: Tofu and Spicy Tomato Sauce

Serving Size: 4

Preparation Time: 15 minutes

Cooking Time: 35 minutes

Ingredients:

- 1 tablespoon of oyster-flavored sauce
- 1 teaspoon of chili garlic sauce
- 1 tablespoon of cooking oil
- 2 small tomatoes, cut into 3/4-inch cubes
- 1 teaspoon of garlic, minced
- 1 teaspoon of minced ginger
- 1/3 cup of chicken broth
- ¼ cup of ketchup
- 1 small zucchini, half lengthwise, and then roll cut
- 1 package (16 ounces) regular tofu, drained and cut into half-inch cubes

Directions:

1. Combine the ketchup, chicken broth, oyster-flavored sauce, and chili garlic sauce inside a bowl to make the sauce.
2. Heat a wok on a high fire and add in the oil to cover the sides. Add the ginger and garlic. Cook, constantly stirring, until the ginger and garlic are fragrant, approximately 10 seconds. Stir in the zucchini and tomatoes for approximately 1 minute, or when the zucchini is tender-crisp.
3. Turn the heat down to medium. Cover and bring to boil about half a minute after adding the tofu and sauce. Remove lid and continue to simmer until the sauce has slightly reduced.

Recipe 93: Tofu and Veggie Scramble

Serving Size: 2

Preparation Time: 15 minutes

Cooking Time: 15 minutes

Ingredients:

- ½ tablespoon of olive oil
- 1 small red bell pepper, chopped
- 1 cup of cherry tomatoes, chopped finely
- 1 small onion, chopped finely
- 1 ½ cups of firm tofu, crumbled and chopped
- Sea salt, as required
- Pinch of cayenne pepper
- Pinch of ground turmeric

Directions:

1. In a wok, heat oil over medium heat and eventually sauté the onion and bell pepper for approximately about 4-5 minutes.
2. Add the tomatoes and cook for approximately about 1-2 minutes.
3. Add the tofu, turmeric, cayenne pepper and salt and cook for approximately about 6-8 minutes.
4. Serve hot.

Recipe 94: Tofu Mapo

Serving Size: 4

Preparation Time: 15 minutes

Cooking Time: 15 minutes

Ingredients:

- ¼ pound ground pork
- ½ sweet onion, finely chopped
- ½ teaspoon of Chinese chili paste
- 1 teaspoon of Sichuan peppercorns
- 2 tablespoons of black bean sauce
- ½ block firm tofu, cut into cubes
- 1 garlic clove, minced
- 2 tablespoons of peanut oil

Directions:

1. Preheat your wok to medium-high. Add in the oil to cover your wok.
2. Stir in the onion, chili paste, and garlic for approximately 1 minute, careful not to burn the ingredients.
3. Stir-fry the pork for 3 to 4 minutes, or until it is nearly cooked through.
4. Reduce to a minimum of medium-low heat and stir in the tofu with black bean sauce. 4–5 minutes of stir-frying makes no difference if part of tofu does not form ideal cubes.
5. Remove the wok from the heat and sprinkle the Sichuan peppercorns over the pork and tofu. Serve over rice, if desired.

Recipe 95: Tofu with Black Bean Sauce

Serving Size: 4

Preparation Time: 15 minutes

Cooking Time: 10 minutes

Ingredients:

- 3 tablespoons of oil
- 2 garlic cloves, minced
- ¼ teaspoon of sugar
- 2 scallions, whites and greens, separated
- 3 dried red chilies, deseeded and chopped
- 1 tablespoon of Shaoxing wine
- 1 pound of firm tofu, diced
- ½ tablespoon of light soy sauce
- ½ teaspoon of sesame oil
- ¼ teaspoon of ground white pepper
- 2 tablespoons of fermented black beans, rinsed
- 1 teaspoon of cornstarch
- 2 tablespoons of water

Directions:

1. Sauté the garlic with oil in a large wok for 30 seconds.
2. Stir in the tofu and cook it for 5 minutes until golden brown.
3. Add the black beans, wine, soy sauce, red chilies, white pepper, and sugar.
4. Next, cover to cook for approximately about 3 minutes.
5. Stir in the cornstarch, mix well, and cook for approximately about 2 minutes.
6. Garnish with scallions. Serve warm.

Recipe 96: Twice-Cooked Chile Pork

Serving Size: 3

Preparation Time: 25 minutes

Cooking Time: 1 hour and 17 minutes

Ingredients:

- 11 oz. skin-on, boneless pork belly
- 2 teaspoons of sweet bean paste
- 1/4 teaspoon of white sugar
- 1 slice of fresh ginger, lightly smashed
- 1/4 teaspoon of Sichuan peppercorns
- 3 tablespoons of vegetable oil, divided
- 1 green bell pepper, 3/4-inch pieces
- 1 1/2 tablespoons of chile bean sauce (toban djan)
- 1/4 teaspoon of salt

Directions:

1. Put the raw pork belly in a pot and add water to cover it. Toss in the Sichuan peppercorns and ginger then simmer on medium-high heat. Reduce the heat to a heat of medium-low, cover, and cook for approximately about 20 minutes, or until some of the fat has rendered itself.
2. Remove the cooked pork belly from the saucepan and set aside for 15 minutes to cool to room temperature before draining.
3. Slice the pork to thin slices that are 1/8-inch thick. Put the slices back in the pot then add the sweet bean paste, sugar, and chili bean paste while stirring. Cover the pot and cook for approximately about 15-20 minutes on medium heat until the pork becomes tender.
4. Pour 1/2 teaspoon of oil in a wok and heat it on medium heat. Cook the salt and green bell pepper in the oil for 3-5 minutes while stirring until it starts to soften then place it on a dish.
5. Pour the leftover 2 1/2 tablespoons of oil in a medium-sized wok and heat it on medium-high heat. Cook the pork in the oil for 3-5 minutes while stirring until it starts to shrink and turn brown. Put the green bell pepper back in the wok and cook for approximately about another 2 minutes while stirring, until it's fragrant.

Recipe 97: Vegetable Fried Rice

Serving Size: 4

Preparation Time: 20 minutes

Cooking Time: 55 minutes

Ingredients:

- 3 cups of water
- 1 small yellow onion, chopped
- 1 small green bell pepper, chopped
- 1 cup of frozen petite peas
- 1 teaspoon of minced garlic
- 1/4 teaspoon of red pepper flakes
- 1 1/2 cups of quick-cooking brown rice
- 2 tablespoons of peanut oil
- 1/4 cup of roasted peanuts (optional)
- 3 green onions, thinly sliced
- 3 tablespoons of soy sauce
- 2 teaspoons of sesame oil

Directions:

1. Boil water in a cooking pan then add the rice while stirring. Lower the heat, cover the pan and leave it for 20 minutes, simmering.
2. While the rice is cooking, put the peanut oil in a large cooking pan or wok and heat it over medium heat. Cook the onions, garlic, bell pepper and pepper flakes in the oil for 3 minutes with occasional stirring.
3. Turn the heat up to medium high heat and stir-fry the cooked rice, soy sauce, and green onions for 1 minute. cook for approximately about another minute after adding the peas. Turn the heat off then pour the sesame oil in and blend well. If you prefer, you can add peanuts for garnishing.

Recipe 98: Vegetable Peking Style Dumplings

Serving Size: 8

Preparation Time: 10 minutes

Cooking Time: 30 minutes

Ingredients:

- 1 ounces of finely sliced bamboo shoots
- 8 wonton wrappers
- 1 ¾ ounces of bean sprouts
- 1 small finely sliced red onion
- 4 tablespoons of vegetable oil
- 1 finely chopped red chili (remove seeds)
- A handful of chopped fresh coriander leaves
- 1 teaspoon of cornflour mixed with water
- 1 ¾ ounces of finely sliced morning glory
- 1 ¾ ounces of finely sliced pakchoi
- Salt and black pepper to taste
- 1 ¾ oz. finely sliced fresh shiitake mushrooms
- Vegetable oil for shallow frying

Directions:

1. Heat ½ tablespoons of oil in a wok and add mushrooms, onion, pakchoi, morning glory, bean sprouts, and bamboo shoots in it when oil is fully hot. Stir fry the vegetables for approximately about 3 minutes or until they are soft.
2. Remove the pan from the stove and add chili and coriander to it. Season with salt and pepper to taste, and put aside to cool.
3. Spread the wonton wrappers on a smooth surface. Place a tablespoon of filling in the center of each wrapper and fold it over, making a semi-circle. Close the edges together with damp fingers, crimping them together.
4. Put the wontons in a steamer with boiling water and cook for approximately about 5 to 6 minutes. Let them cool.
5. Heat the remaining oil in a pan and when it is completely hot, put the wontons in it for shallow frying one by one. Fry until they turn golden-brown on one side. Remove, drain the oil and serve immediately.

Recipe 99: Vegetable Pot-Stickers

Serving Size: 6

Preparation Time: 20 minutes

Cooking Time: 25 minutes

Ingredients:

- 1/2 cups of Bok choy, chopped finely
- 1/4 cup of water chestnuts, chopped finely
- 1/2 teaspoon of oil, sesame
- 1/4 cup of bamboo shoots, chopped finely
- 1/4 cup of garlic chives, chopped finely
- 1/2 pound of tofu, firm
- 1/2 cups of carrot, shredded finely
- 2 peeled, minced garlic cloves
- 1 tablespoon of soy sauce, dark
- 1/4 teaspoon of salt, kosher
- 1 package of wrappers, gyoza or pot-sticker
- To fry: 2 tablespoons of oil

Directions:

1. Drain tofu. Cut in cubes. Mash. Wash & prepare vegetables. Combine tofu with remaining ingredients & seasonings.
2. Lay out a wrapper on work surface. Dip a finger in water. Moisten wrapper edges.
3. Place heaping teaspoon of filling in center of wrapper.
4. Fold wrapper over filling. Seal shut by pinching edges.
5. Heat 2 tablespoons of oil in wok or large sized skillet. When oil has heated, add dumplings carefully. Cook over high heat for approximately about a minute, till golden brown.
6. Add 1/2 cups of water without turning dumplings over. Cover. cook for approximately about a minute so raw filling cooks. Uncover wok. Cook till most liquid has been absorbed.
7. Place pot-stickers on platter with burned side facing up, along with ginger and soy sauce mixture or dipping sauce. Serve.

Recipe 100: Zucchini Frittata

Serving Size: 6

Preparation Time: 15 minutes

Cooking Time: 20 minutes

Ingredients:

- 8 eggs
- 1 garlic clove, minced
- Freshly ground black pepper, as required
- 1 tablespoon of olive oil
- 2 tablespoons of unsweetened almond milk
- 2 medium zucchinis, cut into ¼-inch thick round slices
- ½ cup of goat cheese, crumbled

Directions:

1. Preheat your oven to 350 degrees F.
2. In a bowl, add the almond milk, eggs and black pepper and black pepper and beat well.
3. In an ovenproof wok, heat the prepared oil over medium heat and sauté the garlic for approximately about 1 minute.
4. Stir in the zucchini and cook for approximately about 5 minutes.
5. Add the egg mixture and stir for approximately about 1 minute.
6. Sprinkle the cheese on top evenly.
7. Immediately transfer the wok into the oven.
8. Bake for approximately 12 minutes or until eggs become set.
9. Remove from oven and eventually set aside to cool for approximately about 5 minutes.
10. Cut into desired sized wedges and serve.

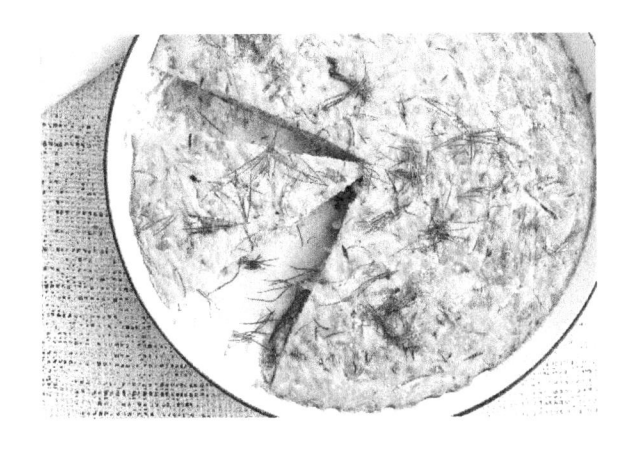

5. Conclusion

A wok may be utilized in a variety of ways. The wok can contain a lot more food, and the high sides enable you to stir swiftly without having to worry about spilling food. It represents the finest purchase you will make in the kitchen because of its flexibility and affordable cost. While everybody understands the wok is necessary for stir-frying, many people are unaware of its other culinary applications. Wok stir-frying is among the most effective and time-saving cooking techniques.

A Chinese wok is an excellent cooking tool because its bowl-like form and sloping edges keep the food in the center, in which the heat is strongest. When cooking in a wok, it's usually a good idea to season your surface beforehand. Make your wok nonstick by pouring oil before cooking and emptying it into a heat-proof container as soon as it reaches smoking temperatures. The wok is highly cost-effective since it can be used more than just stir-frying. It's ideal for deep frying since it uses far less oil than a frying pan. Some people use it to steam food, for example, by placing a bamboo steamer inside. Woks are now a staple in many kitchens. However, most people are unaware of how nutritious a wok-cooked cuisine may be.

Several frying pans are available for buying and cooking in your home. A wok is multipurpose cooking equipment used for deep-frying, sautéing, steaming, and other things. Woks benefit from using less oil in the cooking process, making foods healthier and simpler to digest. It is the most adaptable and useful instrument in your kitchen. Its design ensures that heat is spread more effectively through the base. Because the wok cooks fast at high temperatures, you must keep an eye on it at all times. Cooking with a wok requires a lot of regulated, high heat levels. To hard-sear the meal, the heat should be quite high. Use 15,000 BTU burners or gas burners to achieve the desired temperatures for best results. Using a wok is an essential component of any stir-fry meal. Woks require less oil than traditional pans and are ideal for cooking veggies and tofu. Use high-smoke-point oil to enhance the taste of your meats and veggies.

Made in the USA
Middletown, DE
28 January 2023